CONFIGURING SALES & MARKETING WITHIN DYNAMICS AX 2012

BY MURRAY FIFE

Preface

What you need for this Blueprint

All the examples shown in this blueprint were done with the Microsoft Dynamics AX 2012 virtual machine image that was downloaded from the Microsoft CustomerSource or PartnerSource site. If you don't have your own installation of Microsoft Dynamics AX 2012, you can also use the images found on the Microsoft Learning Download Center. The following list of software from the virtual image was leveraged within this blueprint:

* Microsoft Dynamics AX 2012

Even though all the preceding software was used during the development and testing of the recipes in this book, they may also work on earlier versions of the software with minor tweaks and adjustments, and should also work on later versions without any changes.

Errata

Although we have taken every care to ensure the accuracy of our content, mistakes do happen. If you find a mistake in one of our books—maybe a mistake in the text or the code—we would be grateful if you would report this to us. By doing so, you can save other readers from frustration and help us improve subsequent versions of this book. If you find any errata, please report them by emailing murray@murrayfife.me.

Piracy

Piracy of copyright material on the Internet is an ongoing problem across all media. If you come across any illegal copies of our works, in any form, on the Internet, please provide us with the location address or website name immediately so that we can pursue a remedy.

Please contact us at murray@murrayfife.me with a link to the suspected pirated material.

We appreciate your help in protecting our authors, and our ability to bring you valuable content.

Questions

You can contact us at murray@murrayfife.me if you are having a problem with any aspect of the book, and we will do our best to address it.

Table Of Contents

INTRODUCTION

The Sales and Marketing area within Dynamics AX does a lot more than just track Customers, Sales Orders and Invoices. It has a whole lot of CRM functionality included that that allows you to track **Activities**, **Cases**, **Contacts**, **Prospects**, **Opportunities**, **Leads**, **Campaigns**, and also **Telemarketing Call Lists**.

In most cases, it is just as good as (if not better than) any of the other stand-alone CRM system, especially because you don't need to buy any more licenses, or load any more software, because all of the functionality is delivered with the system.

In this guide we will show you how to all of the base CRM features within the Sales and Marketing area of Dynamics AX.

CONFIGURING SALES MANAGEMENT

Before we start tracking **Activities**, creating **Prospects**, **Leads** and **Opportunities**, and using any of the other cool features that are available within the **Sales and Marketing** area of Dynamics AX, you will want to configure some of the **Sales Management** features so that you can track and report of everything that you will be doing. The Sales Management functions include the definition of your **Sales Units**, the configuration of **Transaction Logging** and also the configuration of the **Statistic** tracking so that you can track all of the queries based around the Sales and Management functions.

In this chapter we will show you how to configure the **Sales Management** features within the **Sales and Marketing** area.

Configuring Sales Units

The first step is for you to configure your **Sales Units**. This allows you to create your reporting structure for all of your sales hierarchies which we will then be able to assign users to, and also associate different responsibilities to so that you can streamline the distribution of activities over the organization.

In this example we will show how to configure your **Sales Units.**

Configuring Sales Units

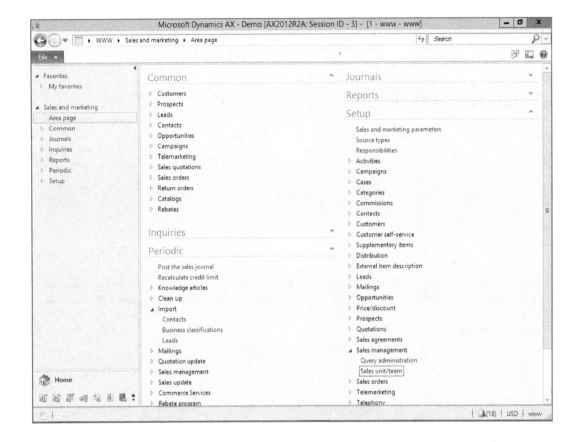

Click on the **Sales Unit/Team** menu item within the **Sales Management** folder of the **Setup** group within the **Sales and Marketing** area page.

Configuring Sales Units

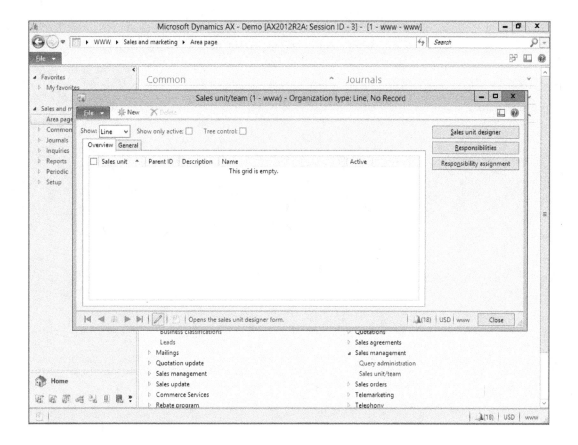

When the **Sales Unit/Team** designer opens, click on the **New** button in the menu bar to create a new sales unit.

Configuring Sales Units

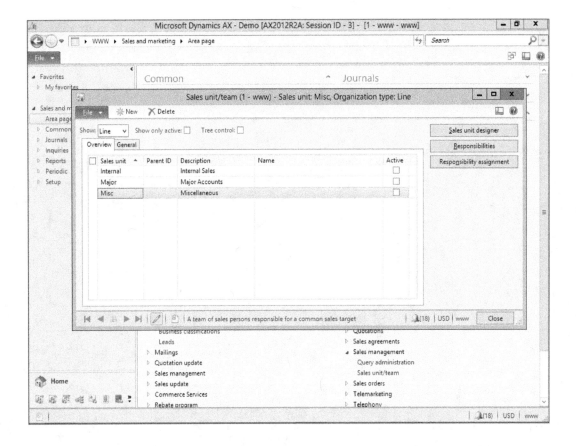

Give your **Sales Unit** a name and description, and repeat the process for all of the base groups.

Configuring Sales Units

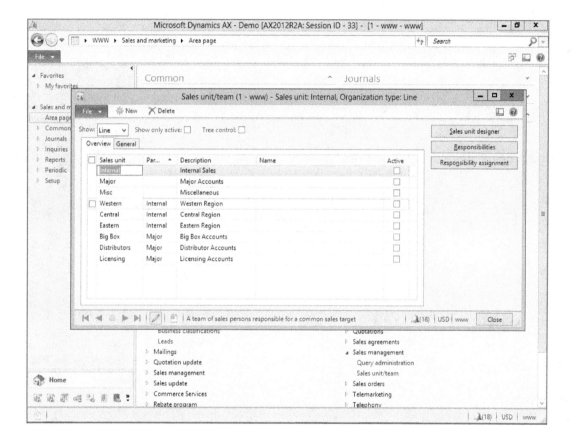

You can also create child groups, by creating the **Sales Unit** and then assigning a **Parent ID.**

Configuring Sales Units

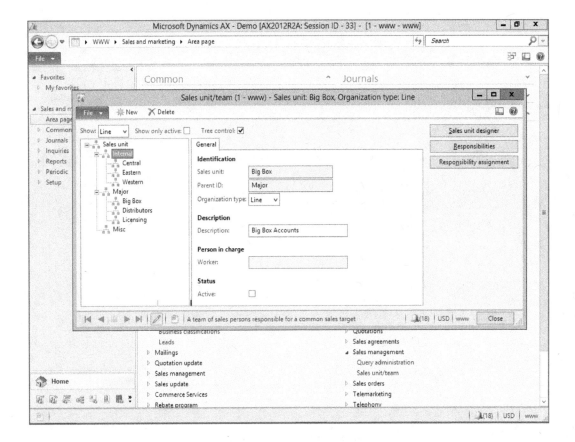

Once you have done this, if you check the **Tree Control** checkbox, you will be able to see the Sales Unit Hierarchy as a tree view.

Once you have finished configuring the **Sales Unit** structure, click on the **Close** button to exit the form.

Assigning Employees to Sales Units

After you have created your **Sales Unit** hierarchy, you will then want to assign your employees to the different sales units. You can do this right from the **Sales Unit** designer and is just a simple drag and drop process. Also at any time, if you want to rearrange the employees, then you just have to move them around within the designer which makes sales administration a little easier.

In this example we will show how you can assign **Employees** to **Sales Units.**

Assigning Employees to Sales Units

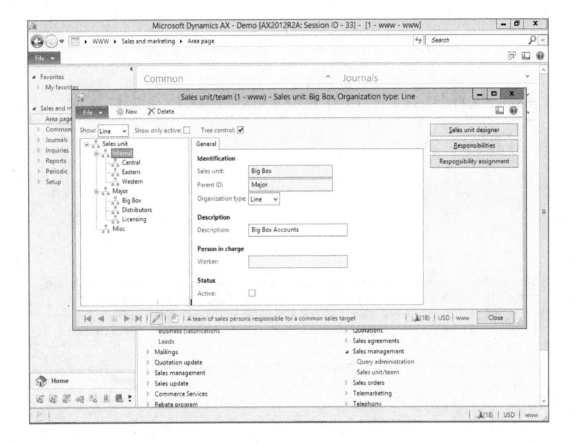

Open up the **Sales Unit/Team** maintenance form, and click on the **Sales Unit Designer** button to the right of the form.

Assigning Employees to Sales Units

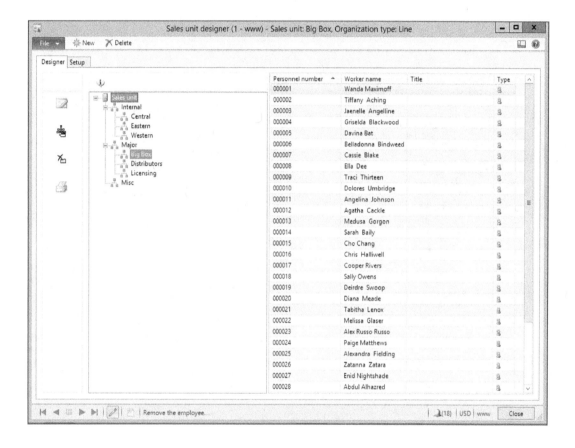

This will open up a designer where you are able to see the Sales Unit hierarchy, and all of the employees within the organization.

Assigning Employees to Sales Units

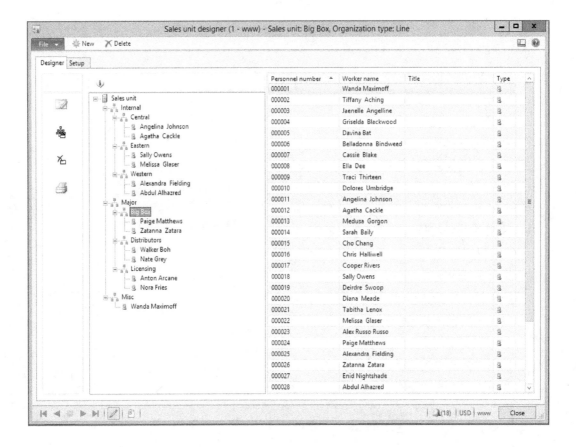

To assign the users to the different sales hierarchies, just drag them from the employee list over to the area of the sales unit that you want them to belong to.

Note: An employee can belong to multiple Sales Units if you like, Dynamics AX will track their assignments, and also have a primary assignment associated with their user.

When you have finished setting up your **Sales** Unit assignments click on the **Close** button to exit the form.

Defining Responsibilities

If you have a number of different groups of people within your Sales and Marketing organization, then you may want to configure the **Responsibilities** within Dynamics AX. This feature allows you to define all of the different areas of responsibility, and then identify the areas within Dynamics AX that they can affect.

In this example we will show how to define your Employee **Responsibilties**.

Defining Responsibilities

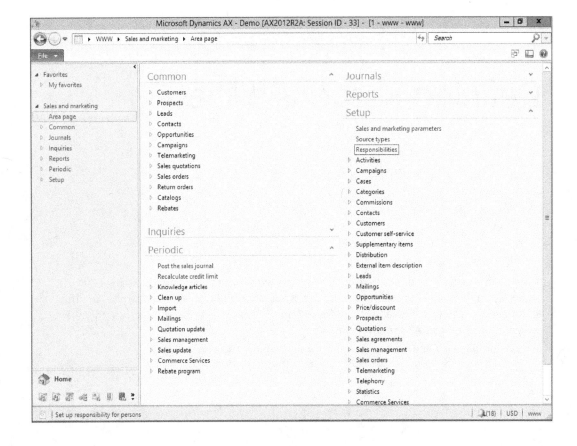

Select the **Responsibilities** menu item from within the **Setup** group of the **Sales and Marketing** area page.

Defining Responsibilities

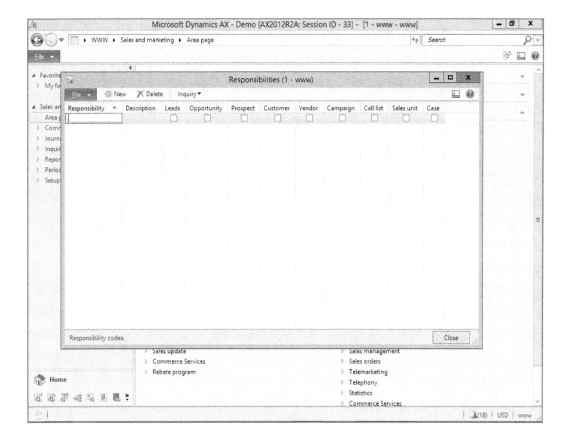

When the **Responsibilities** maintenance form is displayed, click on the **New** button in the menu bar to add a new record.

Defining Responsibilities

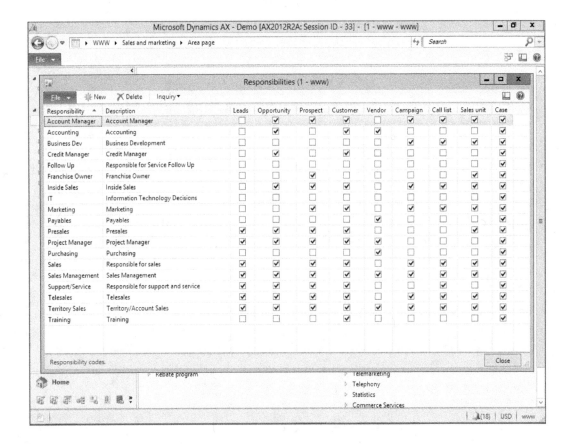

Add the **Responsibility** Name and description, and then identify the areas within Sales and Marketing that they are Responsible for.

Repeat the process for all of the other **Responsibilities,** and when you have finished setting up your **Responsibilities** click on the **Close** button to exit the form.

Assigning Responsibilities to Sales Units

If you define **Responsibilities** within the Sales and Marketing module, then you can take advantage of them by assign them to the different Sales Units. This will allow you to default in Responsibilities based on the Sales Unit that is assigned to the accounts within Sales and Marketing.

In this example we will show how you can assign **Responsibilities** by **Sales Unit**.

Assigning Responsibilities to Sales Units

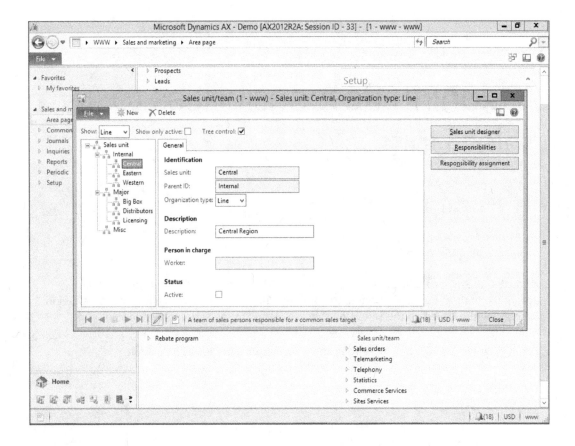

Open up the **Sales Unit/Team** maintenance form, and click on the **Responsibilities** button to the right of the form.

Assigning Responsibilities to Sales Units

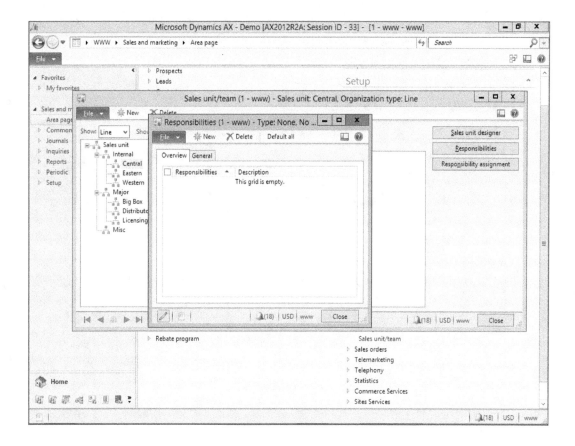

When the **Responsibilities** form is displayed, click on the **New** button within the menu bar to create a new **Responsibility** for the Sales Unit.

Assigning Responsibilities to Sales Units

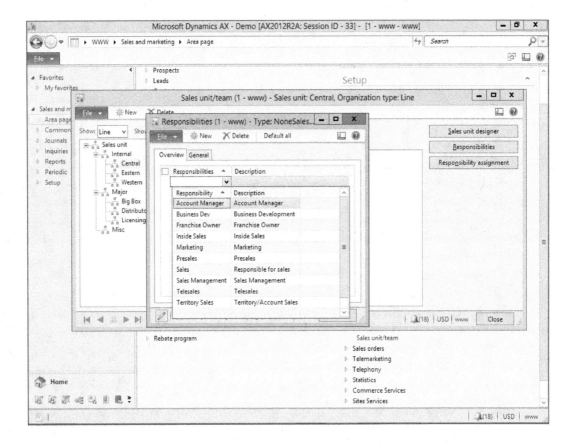

Then select the **Responsibility** that you want to assign to the Sales Unit.

Assigning Responsibilities to Sales Units

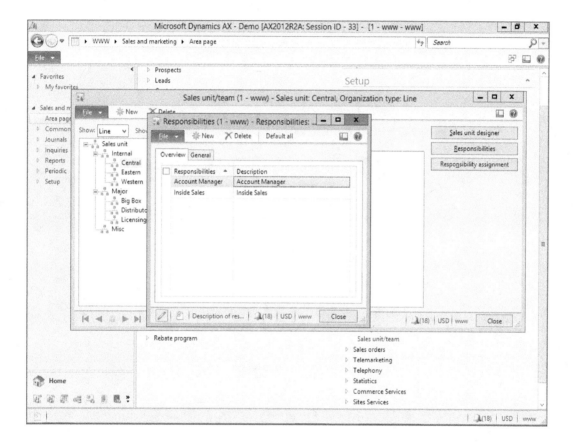

You can repeat this process and assign as many **Responsibilities** to your Sales unit as you like.

Once you have finished, just click the **Close** button to exit out of the form.

Configuring Default Sales Queries

The Sales and Marketing module has the ability to create reports and statistics on almost any information that you would like. The information that is reported off is set up through **Sales Queries**, but you need to load them first in order to use them.

In this section we will show how to load the default **Sales Queries** so that you can start tracking statistics right away.

Configuring Default Sales Queries

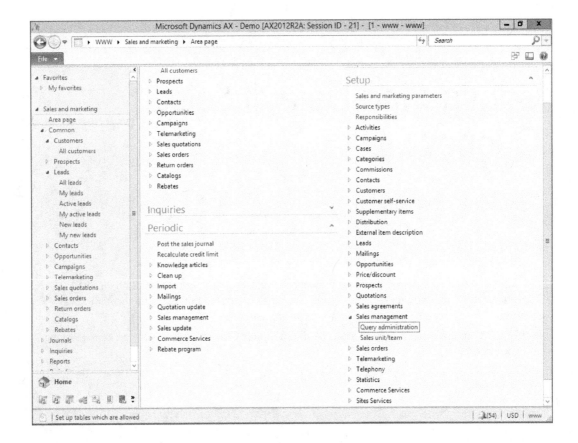

Click on the **Query Administration** menu item within the **Sales Management** folder of the **Setup** group of the **Sales and Marketing** area page.

Configuring Default Sales Queries

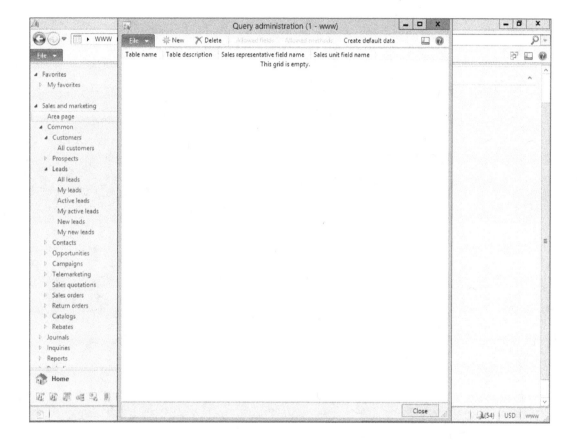

When the **Query Administration** form is displayed, you will notice that there are no **Queries**. To create the set of default queries, just click on the **Create Default Data** menu button within the menu bar.

Configuring Default Sales Queries

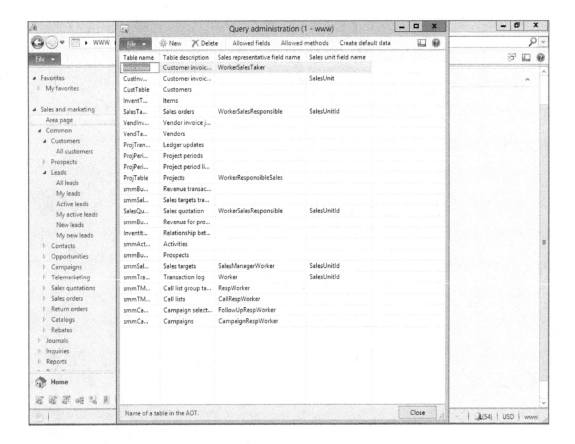

This will load all of the default queries that you can start reporting off.

Click on the **Close** button to exit the form.

Configuring The Default Management Statistics

Once you have your Queries configured you can configure the **Management Statistics** that you would like to track and create reports from. You can create your own custom **Management Statistics** later on, but for now we will just create the default statistics.

In this example we will show how you can configure the default **Management Statistics** from the **Sales Queries**.

Configuring The Default Management Statistics

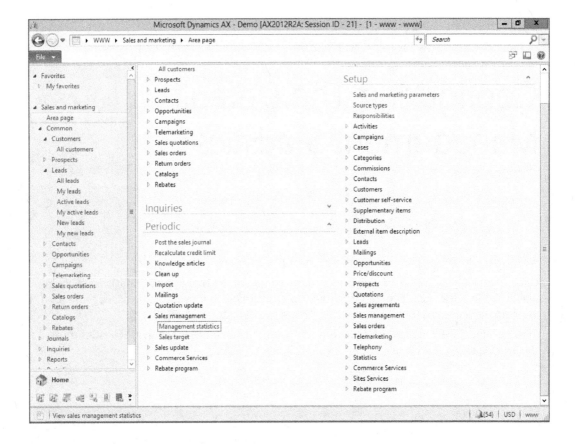

Select the **Management Statistics** menu item from within the **Sales Management** folder of the **Periodic** group within the **Sales and Marketing** area page.

Configuring The Default Management Statistics

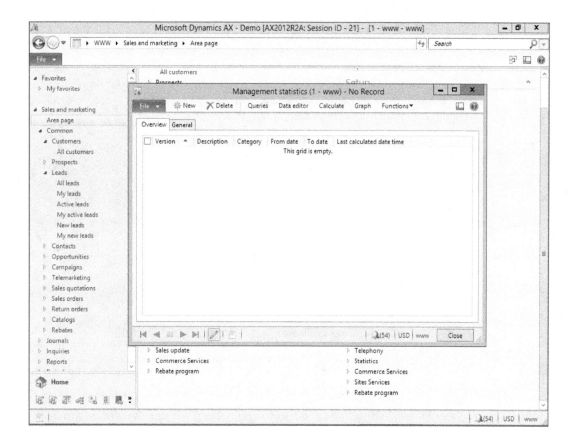

When the **Management Statistics** maintenance form is displayed, click on the **New** button within the menu bar.

Configuring The Default Management Statistics

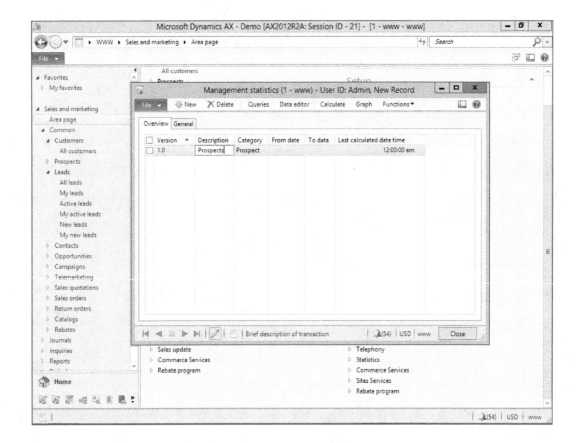

Give your **Management Statistic** a version number, a **Description**, and then select the **Category** from the dropdown box.

Configuring The Default Management Statistics

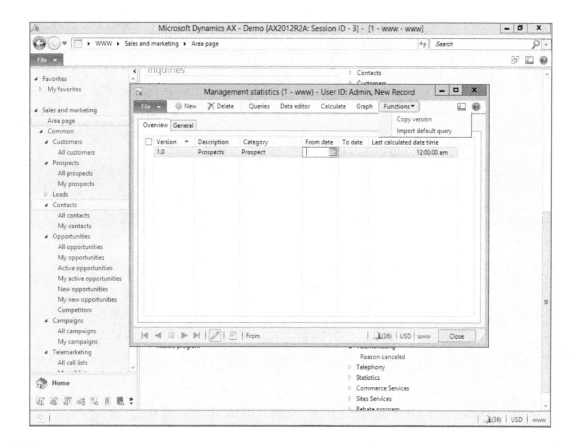

Then click on the **Function** menu button and select the **Import default query** menu item to pull in all of the queries that are associated with the **Category** that you selected.

Configuring The Default Management Statistics

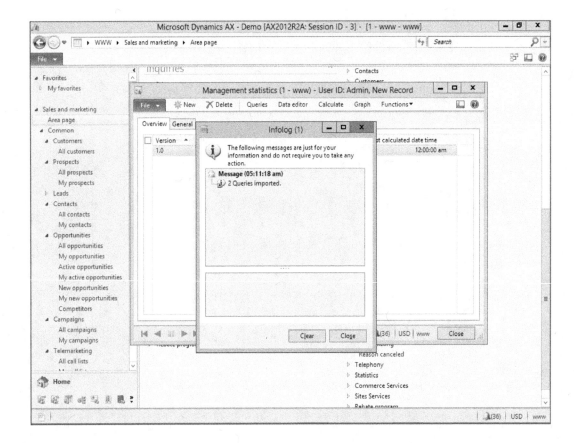

Dynamics AX will tell you how many **Queries** were imported, and you can close the InfoBox.

Configuring The Default Management Statistics

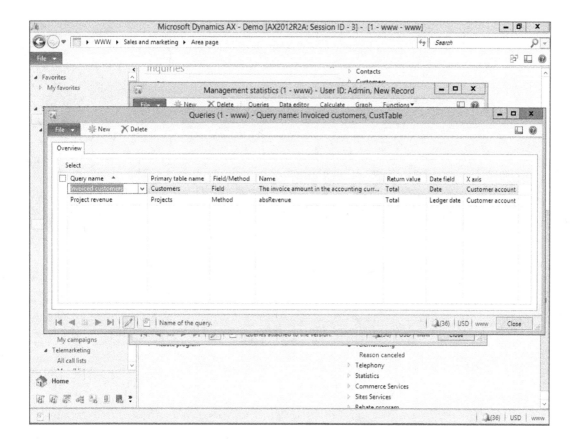

If you click on the **Queries** button on the menu bar, you will be able to see the queries that were imported for the **Management Statistic Category.**

Configuring The Default Management Statistics

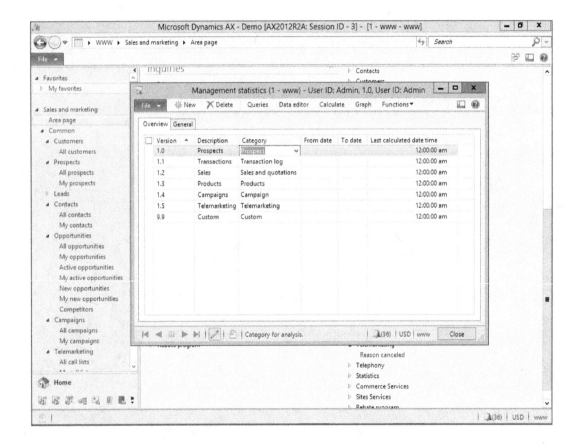

Repeat the process for all of the other **Categories**.

Configuring The Default Management Statistics

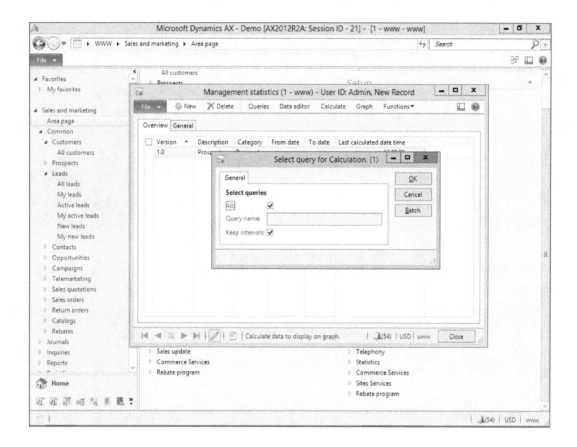

If you want to test the **Management Statistics**, just click on the **Calculate** menu button on the **Management Statistics** form, and click **OK** button on the **Select Query for Calculation**.

Configuring The Default Management Statistics

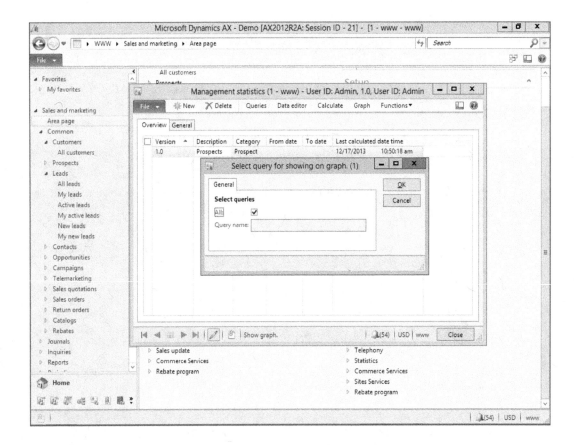

Then click on the **Graph** menu button on the **Management Statistics** form, and click **OK** button on the **Select Query for Showing Graph**.

Configuring The Default Management Statistics

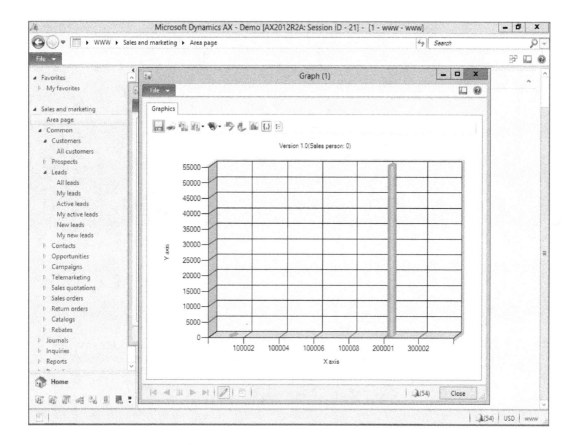

This will open up a graph showing the **Management Statistic** that you selected.

Note: You can also change the graph style here so that it is a little more exciting than a simple bar chart.

Configuring Transaction Logging

One final tool that you may want to configure within the Sales and Marketing area is the **Transaction** Logging. This allows you to track any or all of the transactions and activities that are performed within the system. It is a useful tool for auditing the activity within accounts, and also for reporting on after the fact.

In this example we will show how you can configure the **Transaction Logging** feature within **Sales and Marketing**.

Configuring Transaction Logging

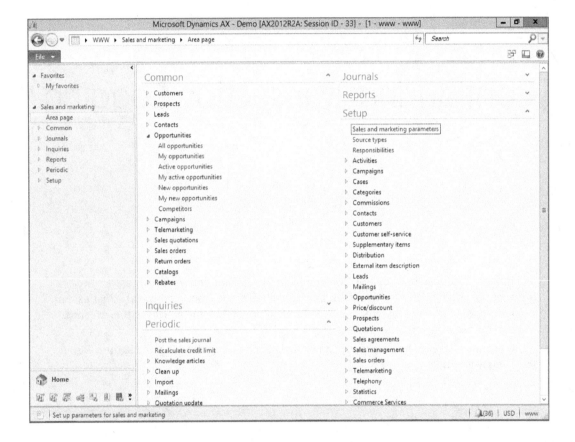

Click on the **Sales and Marketing Parameters** menu item within the **Setup** group of the **Sales and Marketing** area page.

Configuring Transaction Logging

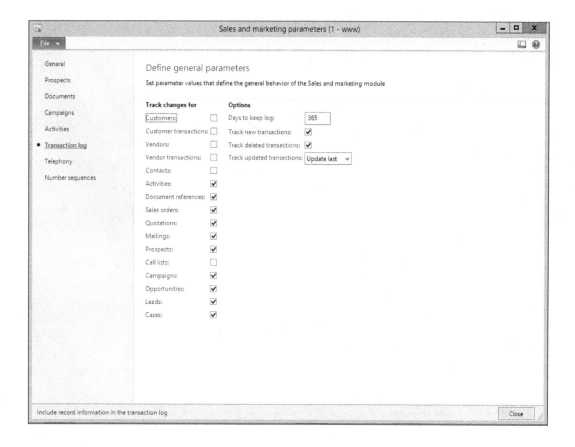

When the **Sales and Marketing Parameters** form is displayed, select the **Transaction Log** tab.

Configuring Transaction Logging

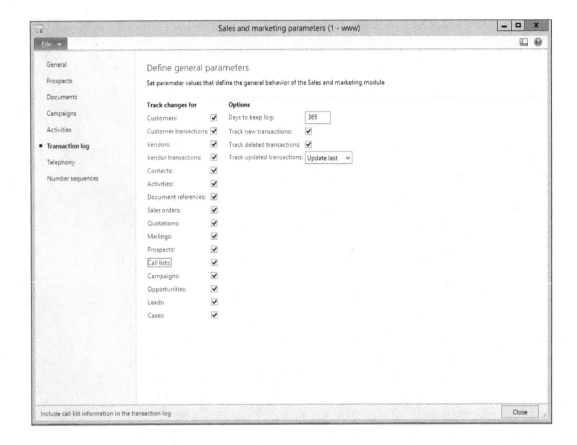

Check any or all of the data elements that you want to track, and then click the **Close** button to exit from the form.

Configuring Transaction Logging

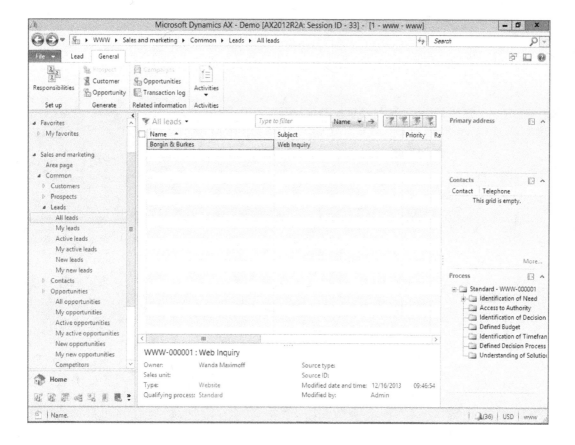

To view all of the transactions that have been logged against the accounts within Sales And Marketing, just click on the **Transaction Log** menu button that you can usually find within the **Related Information** group on the **General** ribbon bar.

Configuring Transaction Logging

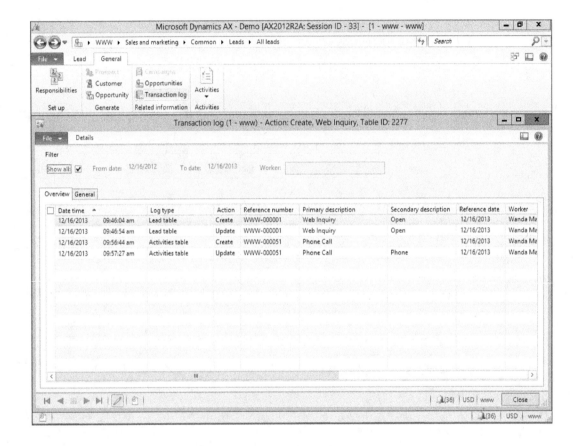

This will open up a **Transaction Log** view that shows all of the logged transactions that you can then drill into if you want.

CONFIGURING ACTIVITY MANAGEMENT

Activities are used within Dynamics AX to track interactions that you have had, are having, and will have in the future, and you can use them almost everywhere within Dynamics AX where a customer, or vendor show up in the system. Before we start using Activities though there is a little bit of data that needs to be configures within Dynamics AX.

In the following chapter we will show how to configure and use Activities within Dynamics AX.

Defining Activity Types

The first step is to define the **Activity Types** that are used within Dynamics AX to segregate out the different activities, and also allow you to track the different ways that you may be interacting with the contacts.

In this section we will show how to define typical **Activity Types.**

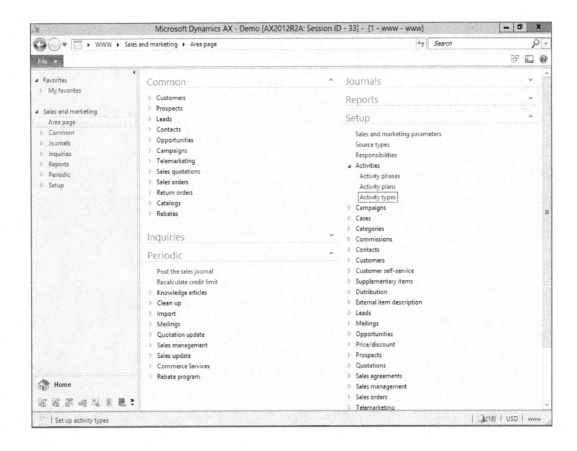

Select the **Activity Types** menu item from the **Activities** folder within the **Setup** group of the **Sales and Marketing** area page.

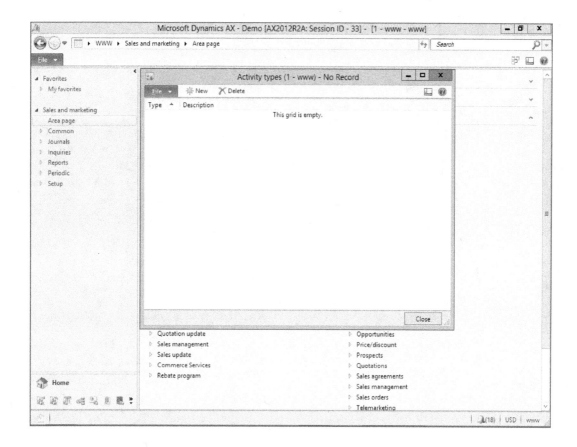

When the **Activity Types** maintenance form is displayed, click on the **New** button in the menu bar to add a new record.

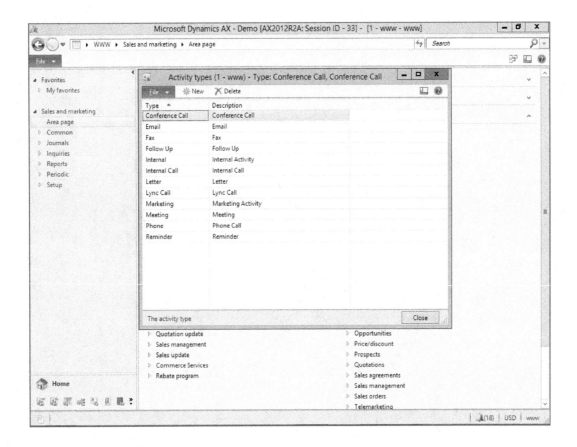

Add the **Activity Type** and **Description,** and then repeat until you have entered all of the **Activity Types**.

When you have finished setting up your **Activity Types** click on the **Close** button to exit the form.

Defining Activity Phases

Now we want to define your Activity Phases. These are used to indicate the current status that the activity is in and can be used to track the progress of the activities Dynamics AX.

In the following section we will show how to configure **Activity Phases**.

Defining Activity Phases

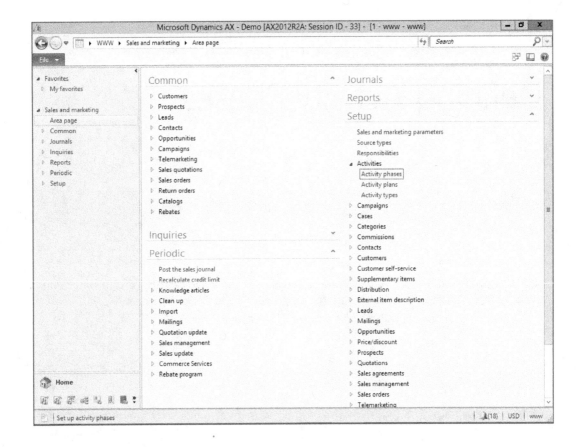

Select the **Activity Phases** menu item from the **Activities** folder within the **Setup** group of the **Sales and Marketing** area page.

Defining Activity Phases

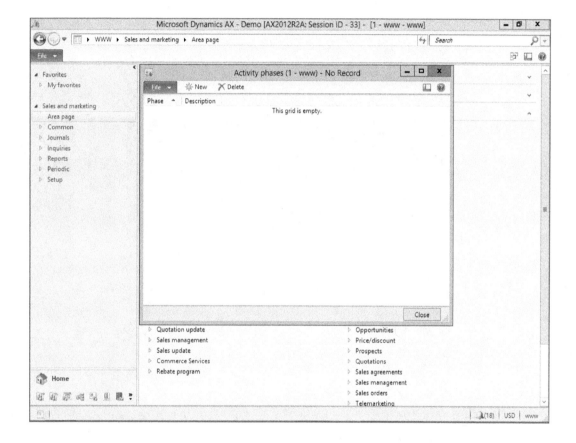

When the **Activity Phases** maintenance form is displayed, click on the **New** button in the menu bar to add a new record.

Defining Activity Phases

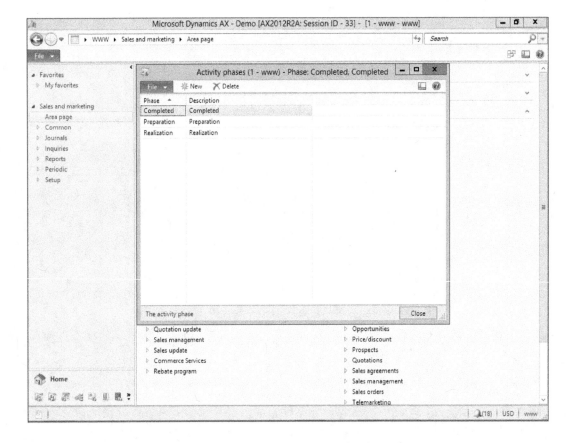

When you have finished setting up your **Activity Phases** click on the **Close** button to exit the form.

Defining Activity Plans

If you want to have activities that are part of a common plan or process, then you can define **Activity Plans** and use them to group activities. When you create activities this will then be an additional classification that you will be able to use.

In the following example we will show you how to define **Activity Plans**.

Defining Activity Plans

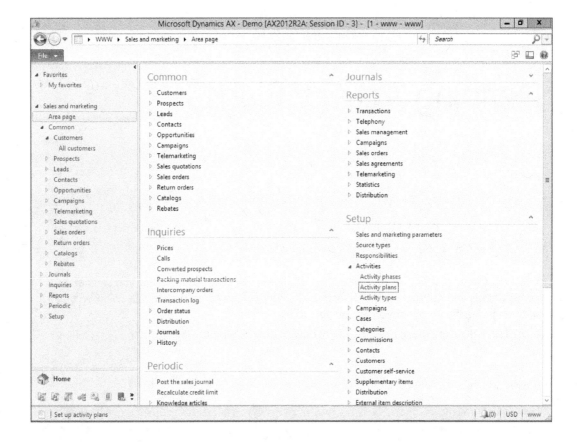

Select the **Activity Plans** menu item from the **Activities** folder within the **Setup** group of the **Sales and Marketing** area page.

Defining Activity Plans

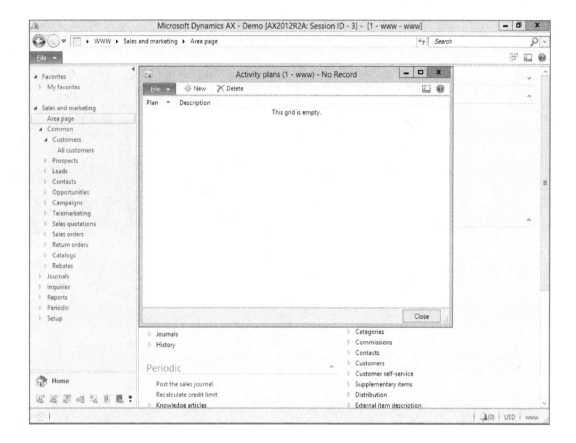

When the **Activity Plans** maintenance form is displayed, click on the **New** button in the menu bar to add a new record.

Defining Activity Plans

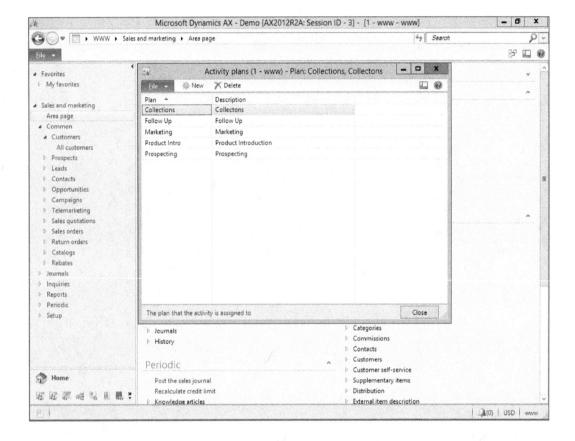

When you have finished setting up your **Activity Plans** click on the **Close** button to exit the form.

Configuring Activity Defaults

Finally we will want to tweak some of the defaults within your **Sales and Marketing Parameters** in order to get the most out of your activities.

In this section we will show how to configure your Activity defaults within your Sales and Marketing parameters.

Configuring Activity Defaults

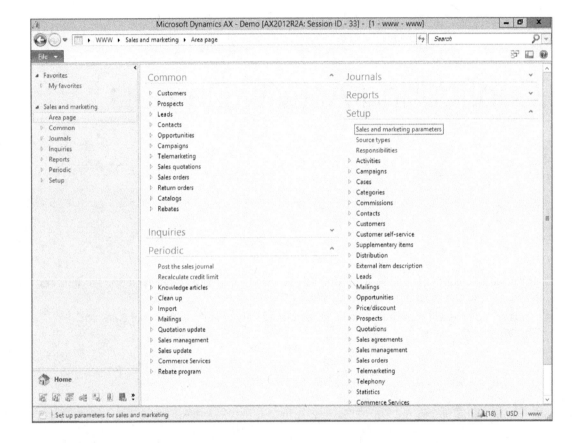

Select the **Sales and marketing parameters** menu item from within the **Setup** group of the **Sales and Marketing** area page.

Configuring Activity Defaults

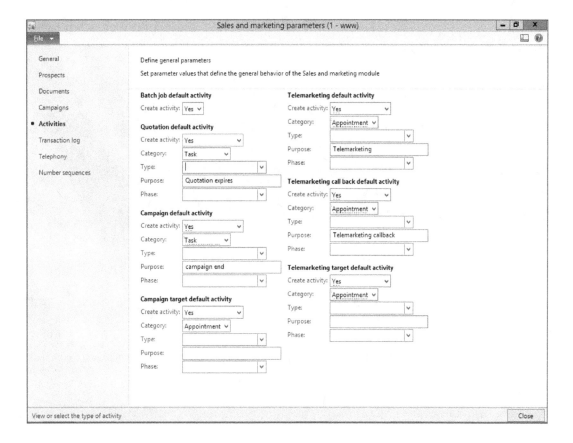

When the **Sales and marketing parameters** form is displayed select the **Activities** tab.

Configuring Activity Defaults

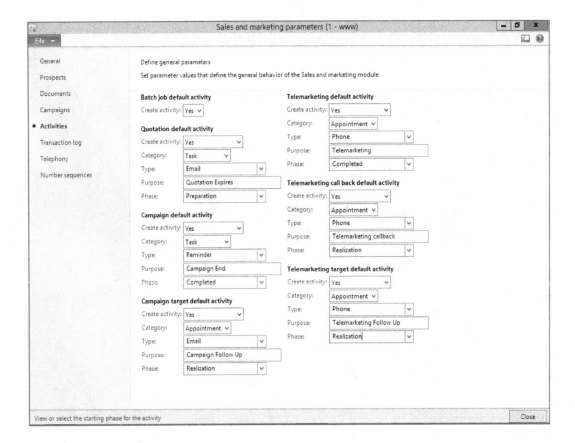

For each of the different activity areas within Dynamics AX, you can specify if you are able to create activities, and also what the default activity type and description will be.

After you have configured your default activity configurations, just click on the **Close** button to exit from the parameter maintenance form.

Recording Activities Against Customers

Once you have configured the activities within Dynamics AX, you can start using them to track all of your notes and interactions within Dynamics AX against customers.

In this example we will show how to record **Activities** against customer records.

Recording Activities Against Customers

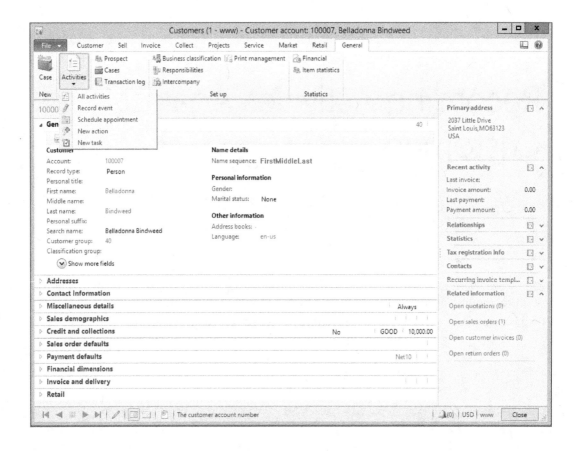

Open up a customer record and switch to the **General** tab. If you click on the **Activities** button within the **Activities** group of the ribbon bar you will see a dropdown menu with all of the types of activities that you are able to record.

Recording Activities Against Customers

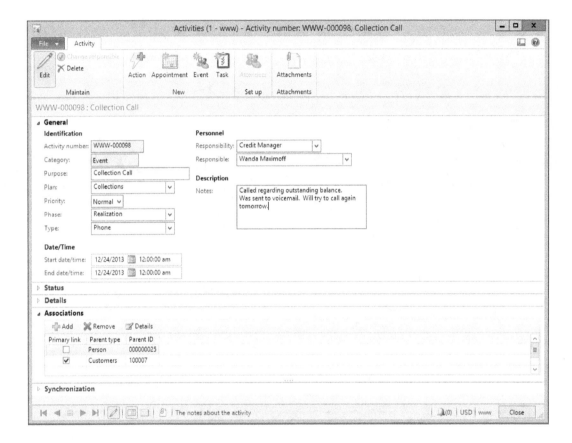

If you select the **Record event** option from the **Activities** menu button within the **Activities** group within the **General** ribbon bar, you can record events or conversations as they are occurring, or after the fact.

Recording Activities Against Customers

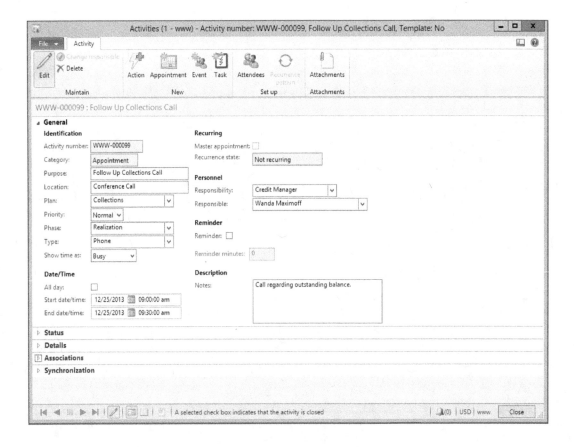

If you select the **Schedule appointment** option from the **Activities** menu button within the **Activities** group within the **General** ribbon bar, you can create appointments that you can then synchronize with your Outlook calendar.

Recording Activities Against Customers

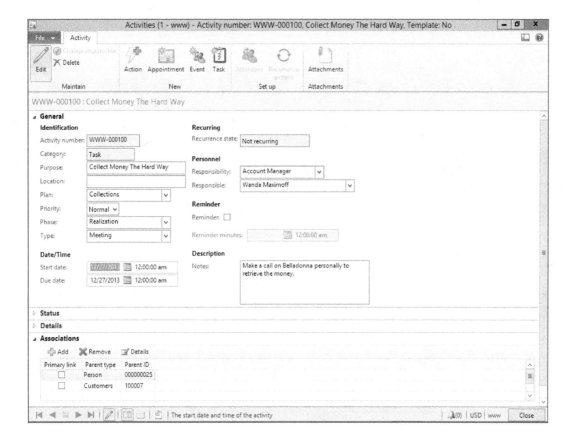

If you select the **New task** option from the **Activities** menu button within the **Activities** group within the **General** ribbon bar, you can create tasks for yourself or other users which will show up as reminders within Outlook when you preform the synchronization.

Recording Activities Against Customers

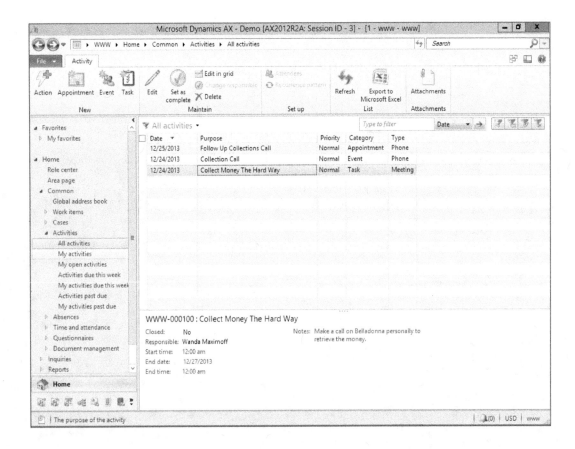

If you select the **All Activities** option from the **Activities** menu button within the **Activities** group within the **General** ribbon bar, you will be able to see all activities that have been recorded against the customer.

CONFIGURING CASE MANAGEMENT

If you want to step up your game a little more than just tracking Activities, then you may want to configure the **Case Management** features within the **Sales and Marketing** area. Cases allow you to record issues and incidents within Dynamics AX, that can be associated with multiple elements such as Customers, Prospects, Products, Vendors etc., and that you can also track multiple activities against. In addition to that, you can create standard process flows for managing the lifecycle of the cases, and even associate workflows with the case management process.

In this chapter we will show how you can configure the **Case Management** to track account issues.

Defining Your Standard Case Categories

There are a number of different types of **Cases** that you will probably want to track within **Case Management**, and each one may have it's own special nuances on how you want to handle them. For example, complaints will be handled differently from new product requests. In order to do this, you will want to configure the default set of **Case Categories** that you want to track.

In this example we will show how you can define your standard **Case Categories**.

Defining Your Standard Case Categories

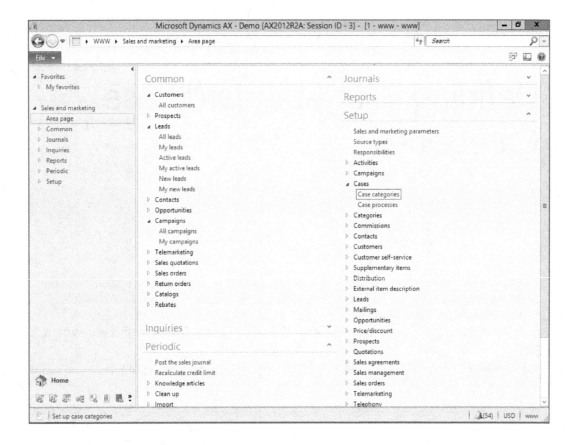

Click on the **Case Categories** menu item within the **Cases** folder of the **Setup** group within the **Sales and Marketing** area page.

Defining Your Standard Case Categories

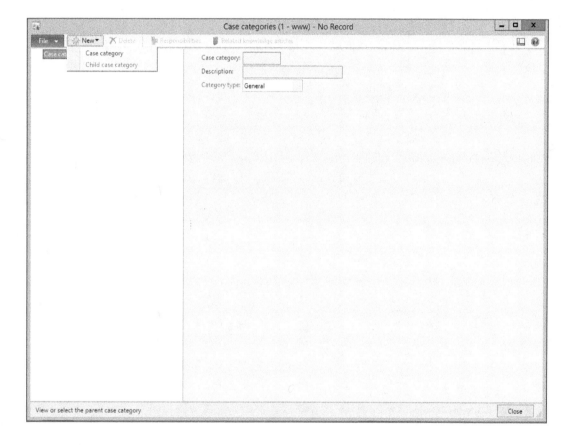

When the **Case Categories** maintenance form is displayed, click on the **New** button within the menu bar and select the **Case** Category menu item to create your first **Case Category.**

Defining Your Standard Case Categories

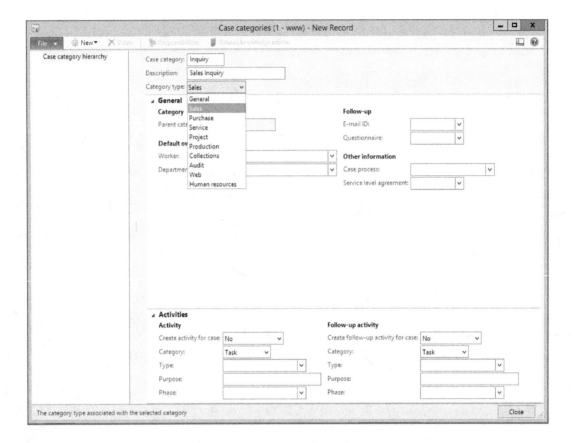

Give your **Case Category** a name, and **Description** and from the **Category Type**, select the **Sales** option.

Defining Your Standard Case Categories

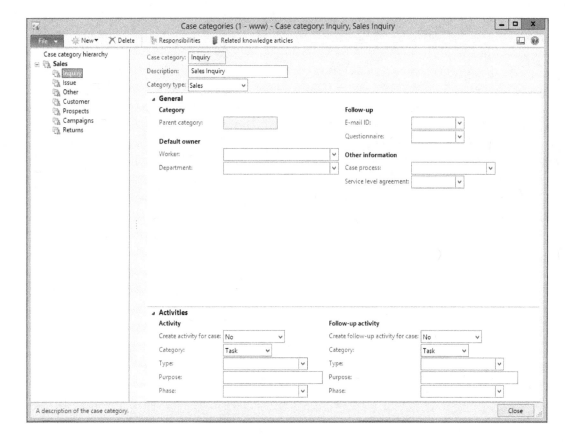

Repeat this process for all of the different types of base **Case Categories** that you want to track.

Defining Your Standard Case Categories

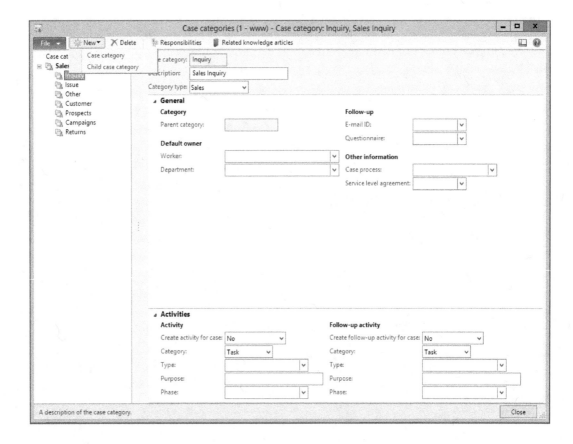

If you would like to create sub-categories of the **Case Categories**, then just select the **Case Category** that you want to use as the parent, and from the **New** menu button, select the **Child Case Category** menu item.

Defining Your Standard Case Categories

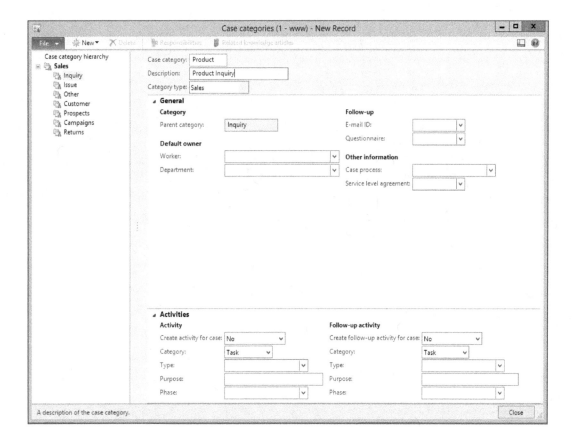

You will configure the child **Case Categories** exactly the same way.

Defining Your Standard Case Categories

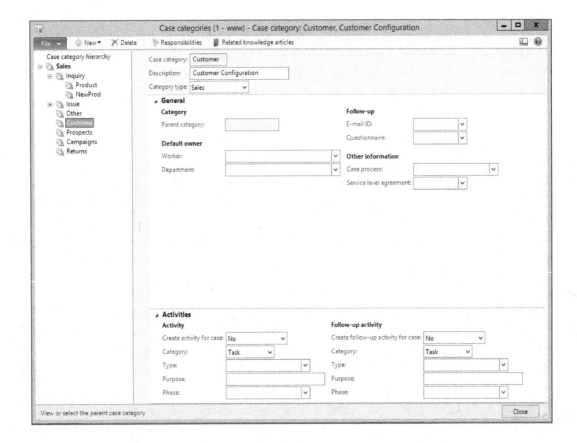

Repeat the process until you have created your **Case Category** hierarchy and click on the **Close** button to exit the form.

Configuring Default Case Processes

If you want to track the statuses of the **Cases**, then you can do that by configuring **Case Processes**. These allow you to specify the standard stages that your **Cases** will be processed through, and also gives you a great way to track the status of all your **Cases** as you report off them. Also, each **Case Category** may have their own **Case Process** assigned to them allowing you to treat them slightly differently if necessary.

In this example we will show how to configure a **Case Process** and then assign it to a **Case Category.**

Configuring Default Case Processes

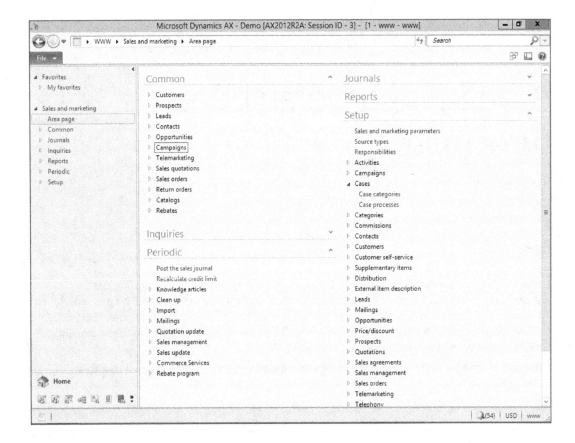

Click on the **Case processes** menu item within the **Cases** folder of the **Setup** group of the **Sales and Marketing** area page.

Configuring Default Case Processes

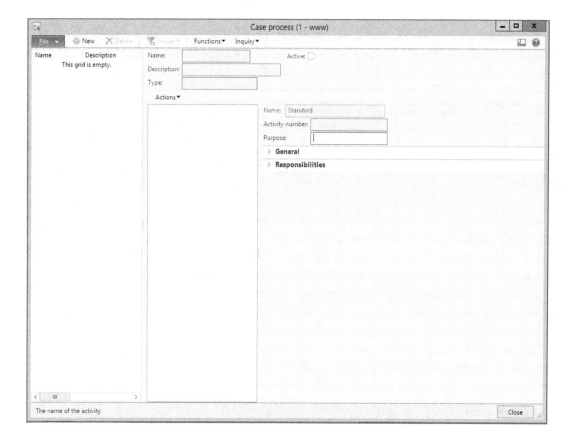

When the **Case Process** designer is displayed, click on the **New** button in the menu bar to create your first **Case Process Stage.**

Configuring Default Case Processes

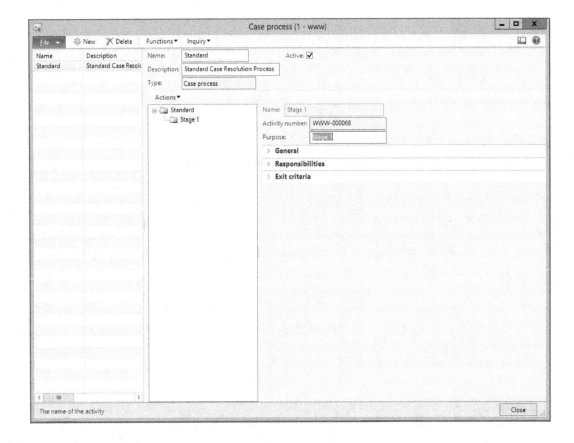

Give your **Case Process Stage** a **Name** and a **Description** and then save it. This will allow you to see the first stage of your **Case Process** in the designer.

Configuring Default Case Processes

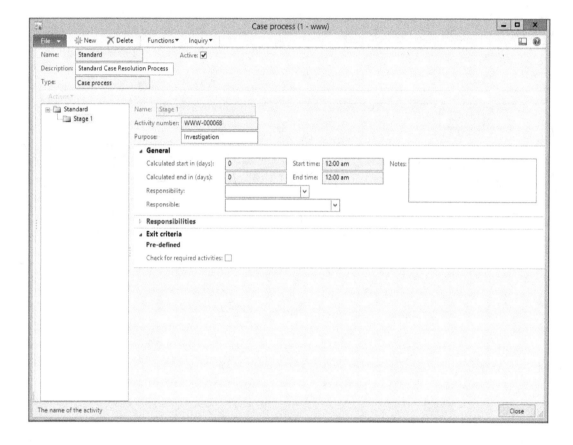

All you need to do is give your **Case Process Stage** a **Purpose** and possibly a description within the **Notes** field.

Configuring Default Case Processes

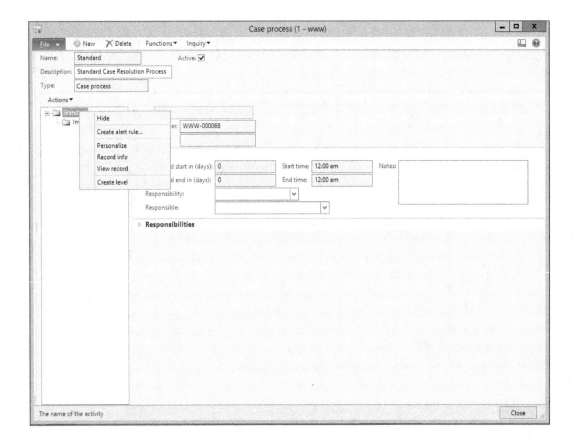

If you want to create another stage, then just right-mouse-click on the parent node in the designer, and select the **Create Level** menu item.

Configuring Default Case Processes

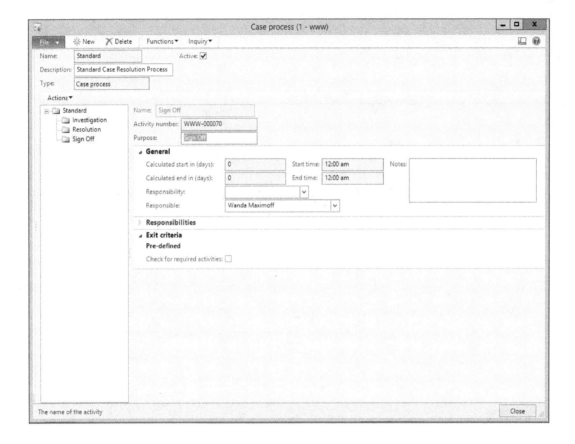

Repeat the steps for all of the stages in your **Case Process**, and then click on the **Close** button to exit the form.

Configuring Default Case Processes

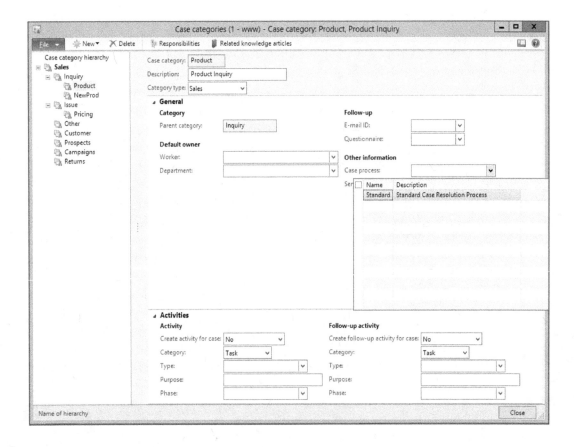

To assign the default **Case Process** to a **Case Category,** just select the **Case Category** and select it from the **Case Process** dropdown list.

Loading Knowledge Articles

If you have a library of common solutions, cheat sheets, and/or standard documentation that you may want to reference, then rather than storing them on a network drive somewhere, you may want to load them in as **Knowledge Articles** so that you can use them during the **Case Management** process.

In this example we will show how you can load the **Knowledge Articles** so that they are available for **Case Management**.

Loading Knowledge Articles

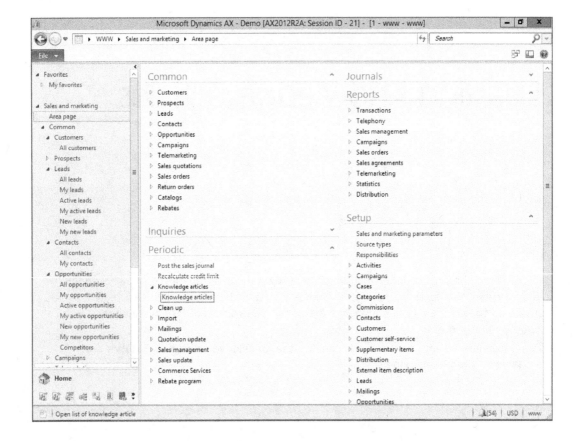

Click on the **Knowledge Articles** menu item within the **Knowledge Article** folder of the **Periodic** group within the **Sales and Marketing** area page.

Loading Knowledge Articles

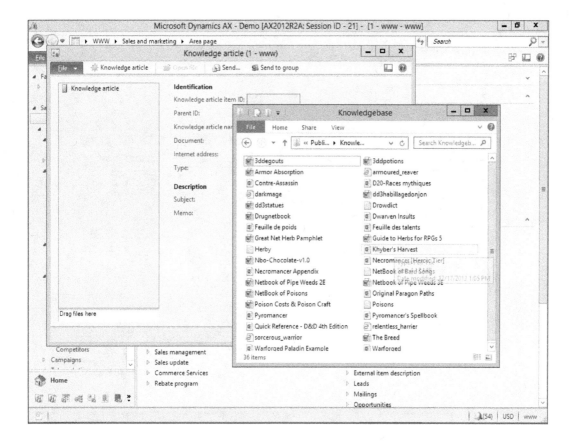

When the **Knowledge Article** management form is displayed, just grab all of your documents that you have filed away, and drag them over into the **Drag Files Here** area in the bottom left of the form.

Loading Knowledgebase Articles

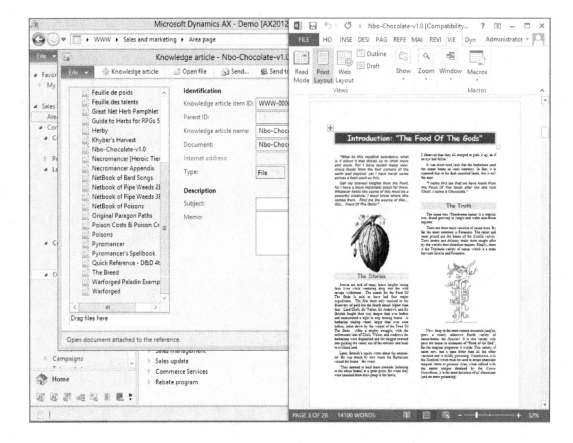

After a few minutes, all of your documents will be loaded within the **Knowledge Article** table.

If you select any of the **Knowledge Articles** and click the **Open Files** button on the menu bar, you will be able to see the document.

Associating Knowledge Articles With Case Categories

Once you have loaded in all of your **Knowledge Articles** then you can associating them with your **Case Categories** so that they will automatically be shown to the users as the **Cases** are being created. This makes it almost impossible to not have the right information at your fingertips as you are trying to resolve **Cases**.

In this example we will show how you can associate **Knowledge Articles** to **Case Categories.**

Associating Knowledge Articles With Case Categories

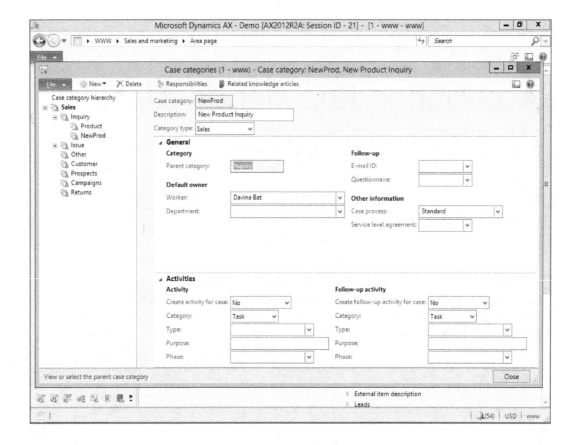

Select the **Case Category** that you would like to add the **Knowledge Articles** to and click on the **Related Knowledge Articles** button in the menu bar.

Associating Knowledge Articles With Case Categories

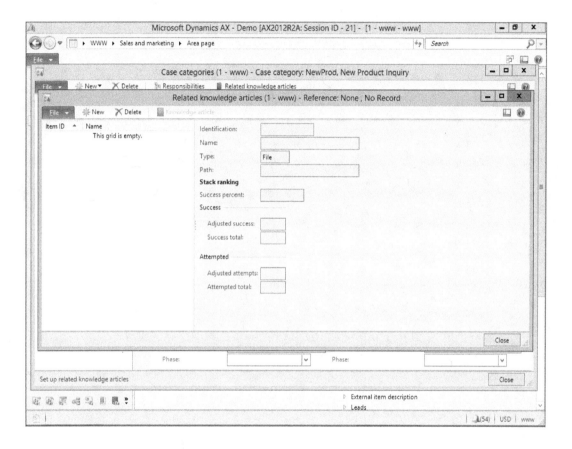

When the **Related Knowledge Article** form is displayed, click on the **New** button to add a **Knowledge article** record.

Associating Knowledge Articles With Case Categories

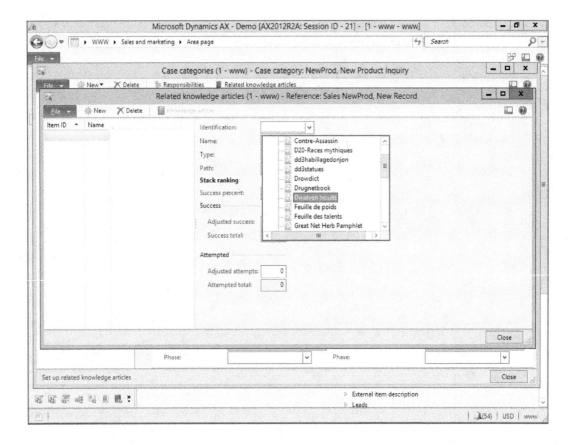

From the **Identification** dropdown box, select the **Knowledge Article** that you want to associate with the **Case.**

Associating Knowledge Articles With Case Categories

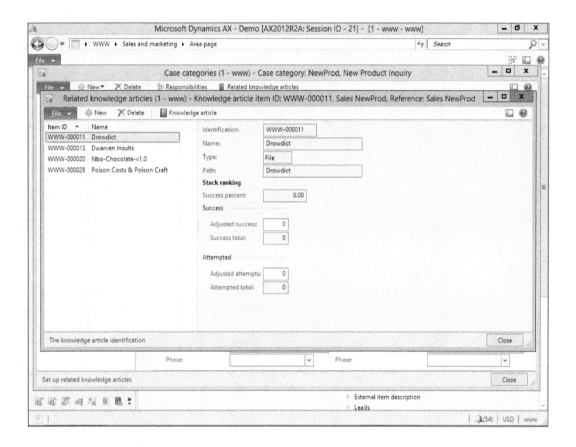

You can repeat the process for any additional **Knowledge Articles** and then click the **Close** button to exit the form.

Creating Cases For Customers

Once you have created your **Case Categories**, then you can start tracking them against your accounts.

In this example we will show how you can create a **Case** directly from a **Customer** account.

Creating Cases For Customers

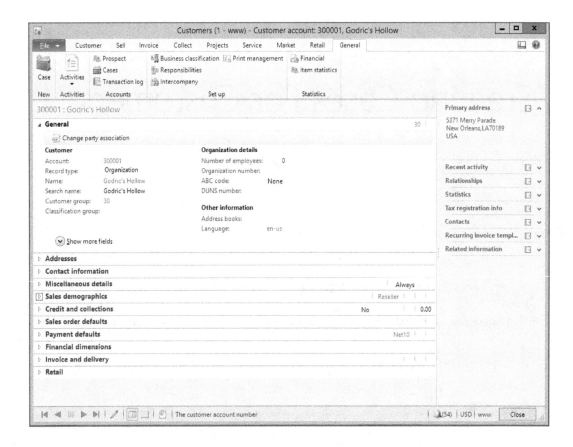

Open up the **Customer** record, and click on the **Case** menu button within the New group of the **General** tab.

Creating Cases For Customers

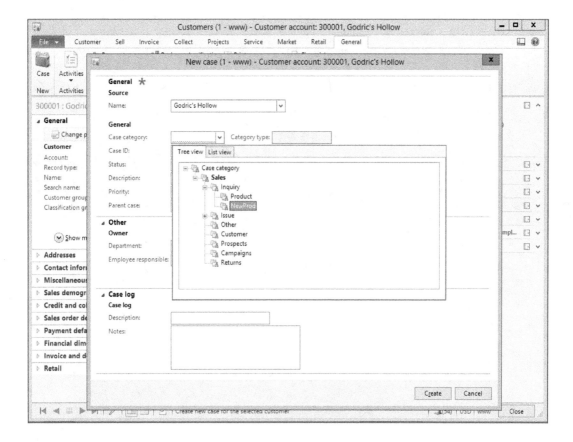

When the **New Case** quick entry form is displayed, select the **Case Category** for this item from the set that you have defined.

Creating Cases For Customers

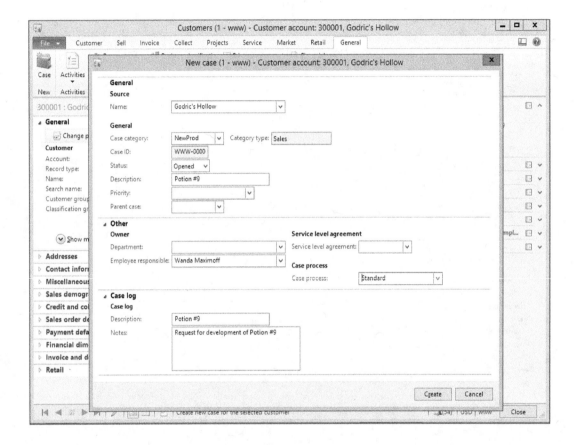

Then add a **Description**, and also any additional notes that you may want to record against the **Case** before clicking the **Create** button.

Creating Cases For Customers

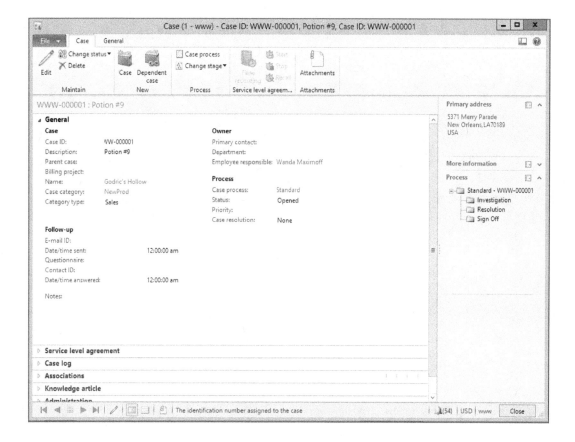

After the **Case** is created, the main **Case** maintenance form will be displayed, allowing you to tweak even more information.

Creating Activities Against Cases

The major benefit of using cases is that it is a way to track all of the **Activities** and **Events** that are related to it. When you are trying to investigate what occurred later on, then this is an invaluable tool.

In this example we will show how to create **Activities** against **Cases.**

Creating Activities Against Cases

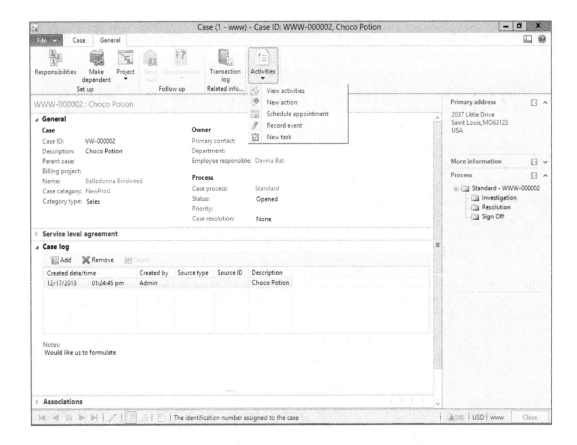

Open up the **Case** and click on the **Activities** menu button within the **Activities** group of the **General** ribbon bar. This will allow you to select the type of **Activity** that you want to record.

Creating Activities Against Cases

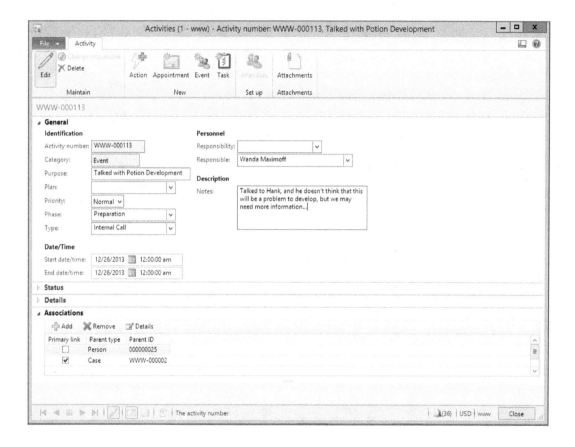

All you need to do is enter in all of the **Activity** details, and click the **Close** button.

Creating Activities Against Cases

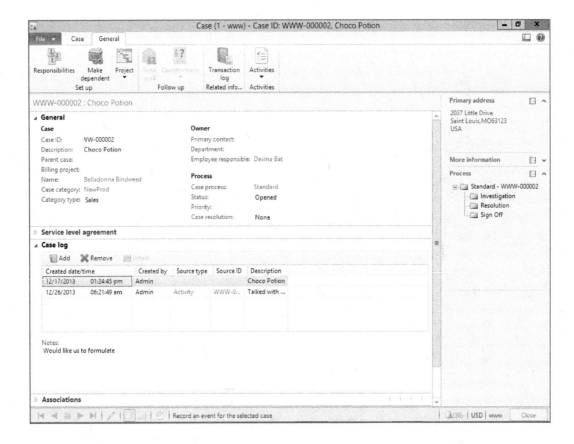

If you expand out the **Case log** tab within the **Case** you will see that the **Activity** is now associated with it.

Using Knowledge Articles in Cases

Finally, if you have associated **Knowledge Articles** with the **Case Category**, then they will be available directly from the **Case** itself. This allows you to open up the documents as reference when trying to resolve the case, an you also have the ability to track if the article was actually useful, so that the next time the **Case Category** is encountered again, you can go straight to the document that has worked in the past.

In this example we will show how you can use the **Knowledge Articles** within **Cases.**

Using Knowledge Articles in Cases

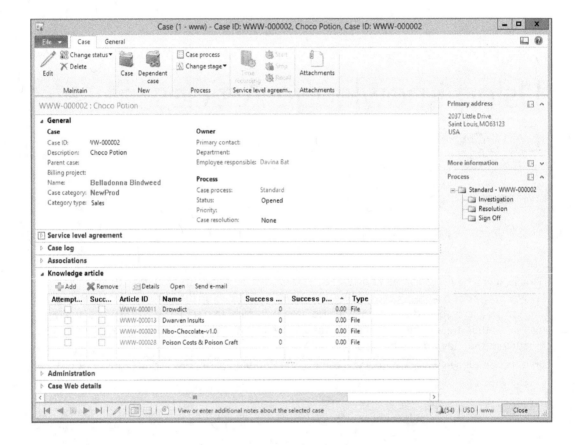

Open up the **Case** that you have associated the **Knowledge Articles** with, and expand the **Knowledge Article** tab. You will see all of the **Associated Knowledge Articles** are listed.

Using Knowledge Articles in Cases

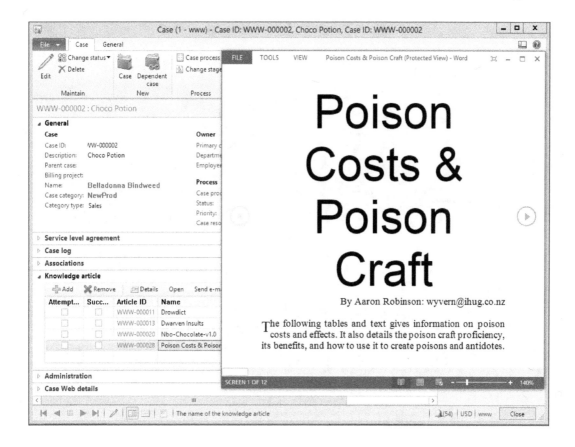

If you click on the **Open** button within the tabs menu bar, it will open the uploaded **Knowledge Article.**

Using Knowledge Articles in Cases

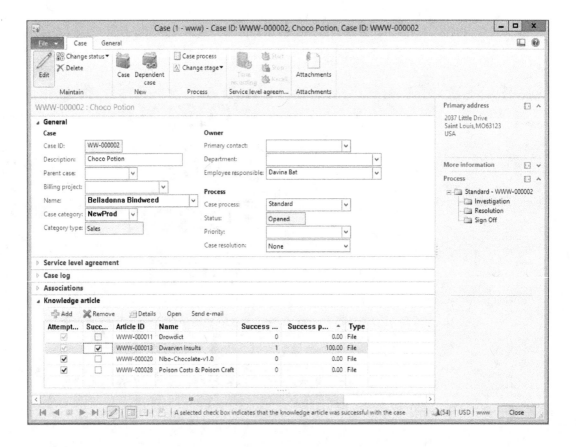

You can also mark the Knowledge Articles to show if you used them or now, and more importantly if they were successful in helping you resolve the case.

Using Knowledge Articles in Cases

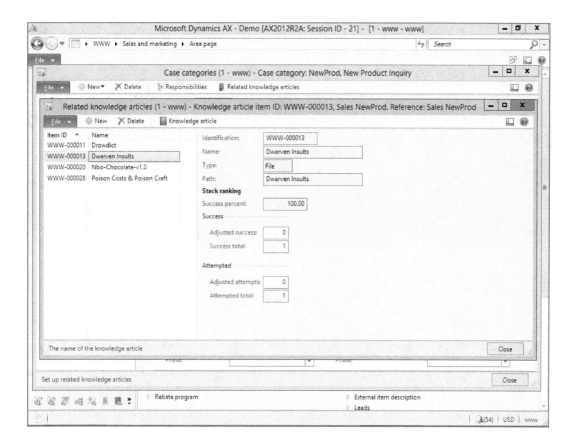

As a side note, when you look at the **Related Knowledge Articles** you will be able to see how many times the **Knowledge Article** was referenced, and how many times it was successful, which is great for reporting.

CONFIGURING CONTACT MANAGEMENT

One of the strengths of Dynamics AX is that it has in-built **Contact Management** in addition to the ability to track **Customers** and **Vendors** as people or organizations. This adds another layer of information that you can track against people because you are able to record all of their personal information without having to record it against the parent records. You can record their personal contact preferences, track activities and interactions against them, and also if they move from one organization to another, all of their history will move with them as well.

In this chapter we will show how you can configure the **Contact Management** within Dynamics AX and start using it.

Define Contact Person Titles

If you want to track the actual job titles of the contacts within Dynamics AX, then you will need to define the **Contact Person Titles**. These allow you to standardize the business titles that you assign to your contacts for better reporting.

In this section we will show how to define the **Contact Person Titles**.

Define Contact Person Titles

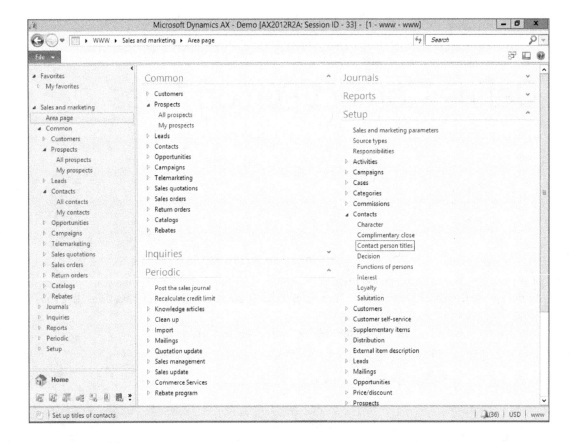

Select the **Contact person titles** menu item from within the **Contacts** folder of the **Setup** group of the **Sales and Marketing** area page.

Define Contact Person Titles

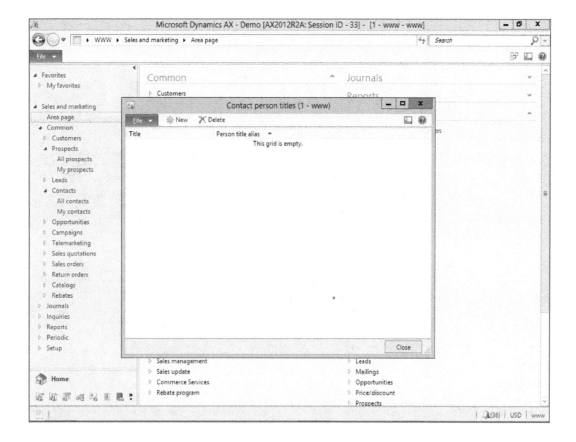

When the **Contact person titles** maintenance form is displayed, click on the **New** button in the menu bar to add a new record.

Define Contact Person Titles

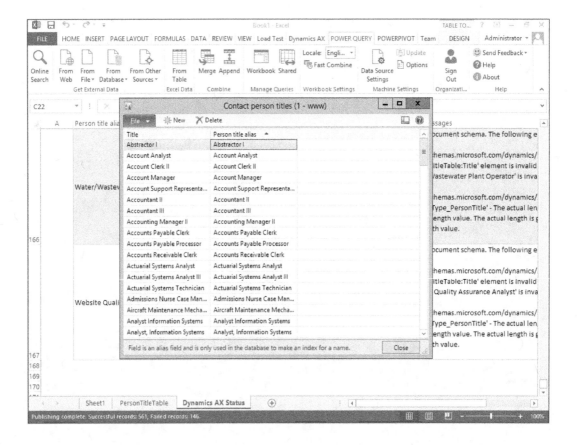

When you have finished setting up your **Activity Plans** click on the **Close** button to exit the form.

Defining Function of Persons

Also you can segregate contacts by the general function within the organization by defining **Functions of Persons**. You can use these job functions later on during when you create campaigns to segregate out your contacts for target marketing.

In this section we will show how you can configure **Functions of Persons** within Dynamics AX.

Defining Function of Persons

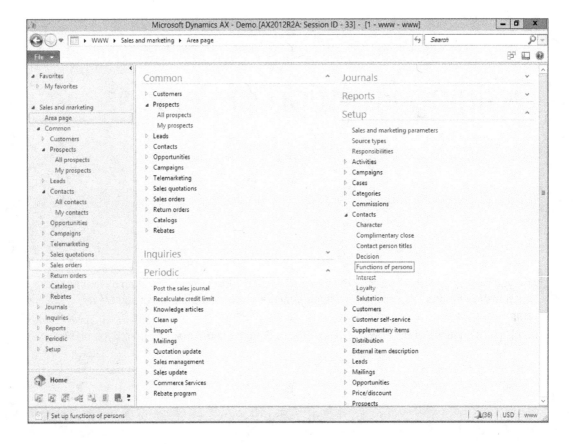

Select the **Functions of persons** menu item from within the **Contacts** folder of the **Setup** group of the **Sales and Marketing** area page.

Defining Function of Persons

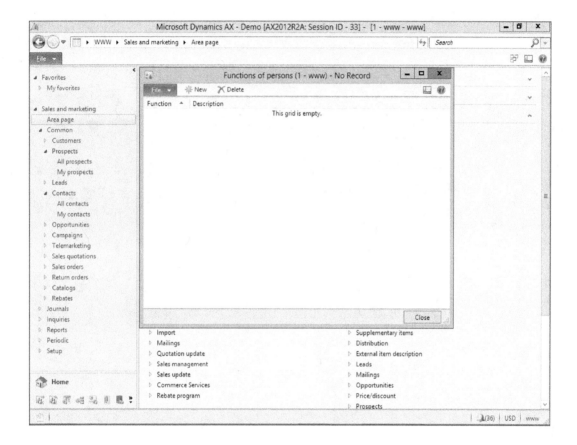

When the **Functions of Persons** maintenance form is displayed, click on the **New** button in the menu bar to add a new record.

Defining Function of Persons

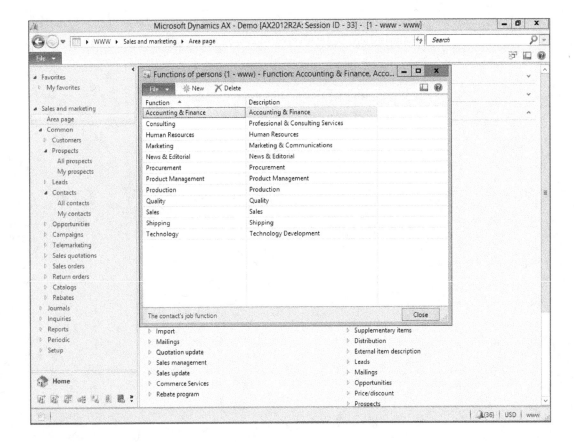

When you have finished setting up your **Functions of Persons** click on the **Close** button to exit the form.

Creating Contacts

Once you have the base codes defined for your contacts, you can start creating the **Contact** records. There are a couple of different ways that contacts can be created, and one is directly from the contact maintenance form.

In this example we will show how you can create a new **Contact** from the Contact maintenance form.

Creating Contacts

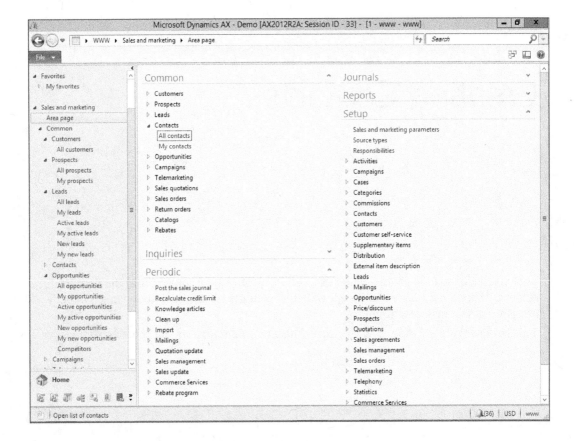

Select the **All contacts** menu item from within the **Contacts** folder of the **Common** group of the **Sales and Marketing** area page.

Creating Contacts

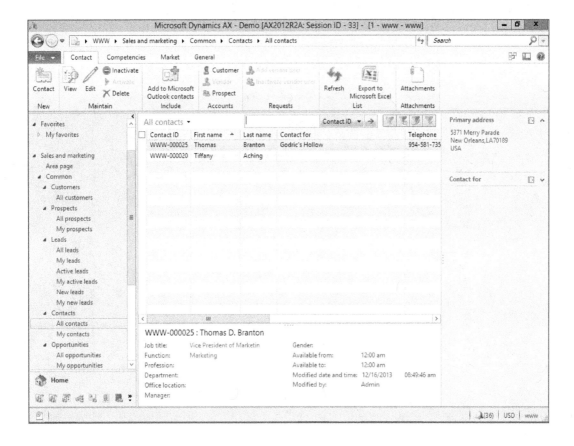

When the **Contacts** maintenance form is displayed, click on the **Contact** within the **New** group of the **Contact** ribbon bar.

Creating Contacts

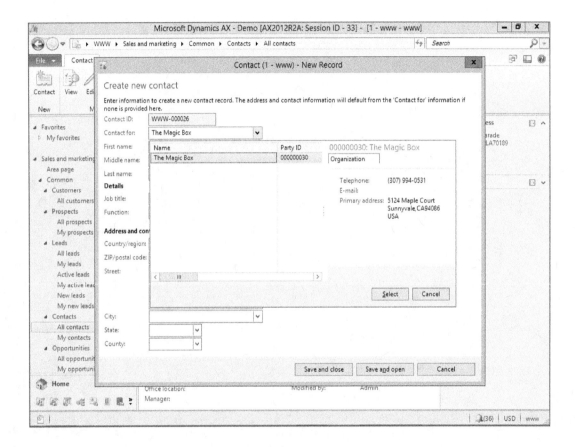

When the **Contact** maintenance form is displayed, select the party that the contact will be connected with from the **Contact for** dropdown list.

Note: Contacts must have a parent record that they are tied to.

Creating Contacts

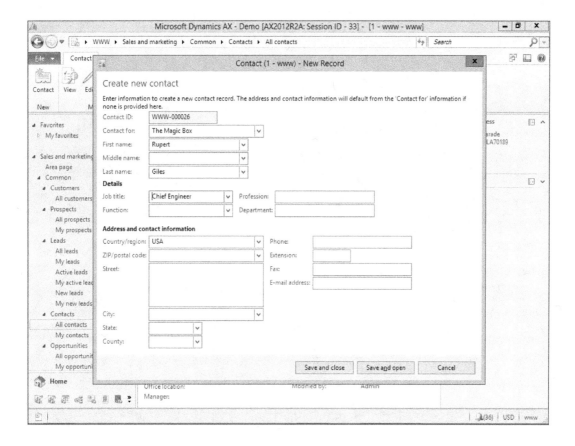

You can then fill in as much of the information as you know about the contact before creating the contact. When you are finished, if you click on the **Save and open** button, it will open up the full contact details form.

Creating Contacts

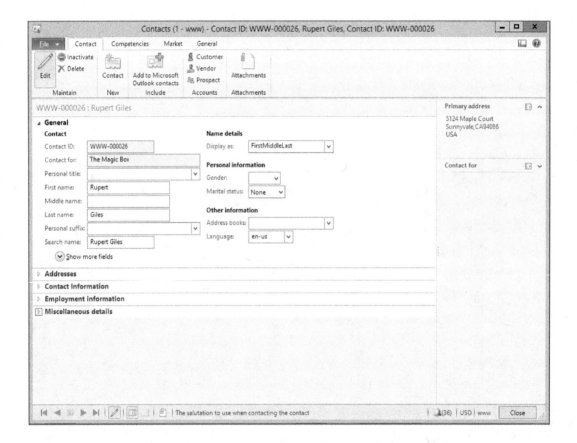

When you are in the full form, you can update any information about the contact that you may need.

Creating Contacts From Customer Accounts

Another way that you are able to create contacts is from the parent records, like the Customers. Sometimes this is an easier way to do this because you may already be within the **Customer** Account.

In this example we will show how you can create a **Contact** directly from within the **Customer Account**.

Creating Contacts From Customer Records

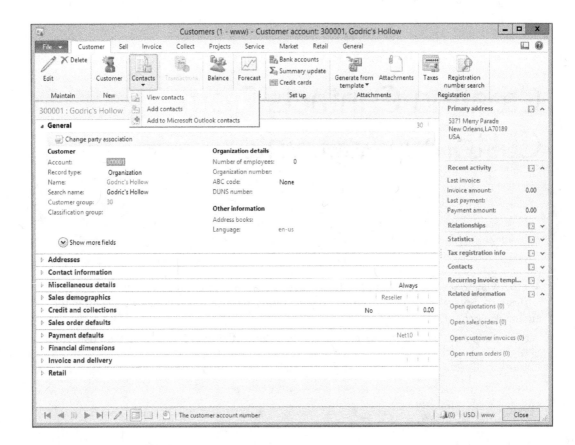

Open up a customer record that you want to add the contact for and click on the **Contacts** button within the **Accounts** group of the **Customer** ribbon bar and select the **Add contacts** menu item.

Creating Contacts From Customer Records

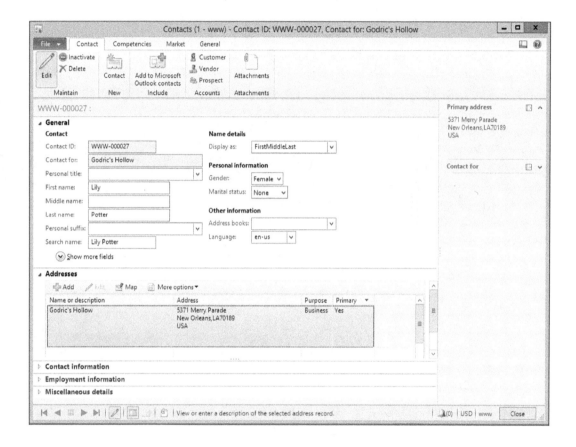

This will allow you to enter the same information as in the previous example, except the **Contact for** will be automatically populated for you.

Viewing All Contacts For A Customer

You can also view all of the contacts that are associated with a customer directly from the customers form. If you are trying to quickly find a key contact then this is a great tool to take advantage of.

In this example we will show you how to view all of the **Contacts** related to a **Customer** account.

Viewing All Contacts For A Customer

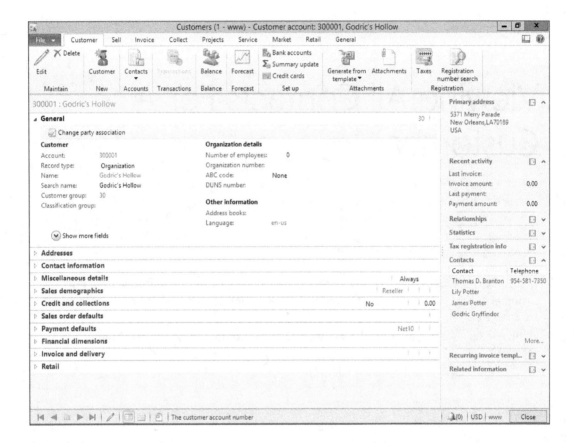

If you open up a **Customer** record, then you will be able to see a summary of the contacts that are associated with the **Customer** within the **Contacts** fact box on the right hand side of the form.

Note: If you click on the **More** link, it will take you to the **Contacts** maintenance form showing you just the records associated with the **Customer**.

Viewing All Contacts For A Customer

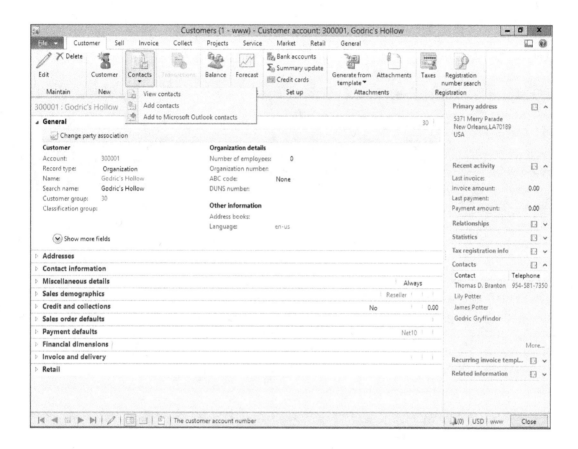

Another way to view all of the **Contacts** for the **Customer** is to select the **View Contacts** submenu item of the **Contacts** menu button within the **Accounts** group of the **Customer** ribbon bar.

Viewing All Contacts For A Customer

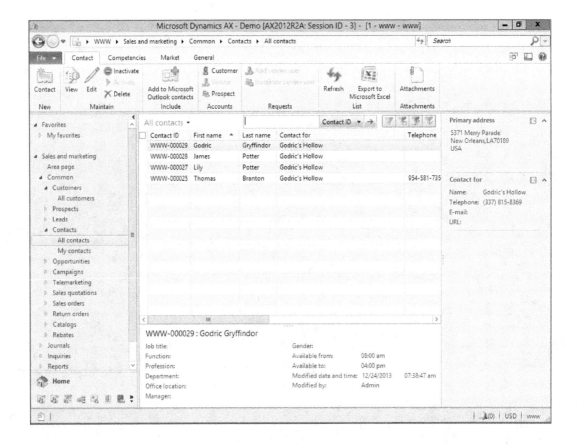

Once you are in the **All Contacts** form you will be able to access all of the information associated with the contacts.

Marking Contacts To Synchronize With Outlook

Dynamics AX has feature that allows you to synchronize contacts with Microsoft Outlook. You don't need to copy all of the contacts within the system though, you have the ability to pick and choose the contacts.

In this section we will show how to mark the contacts that you want to Synchronize with Outlook.

Marking Contacts To Synchronize With Outlook

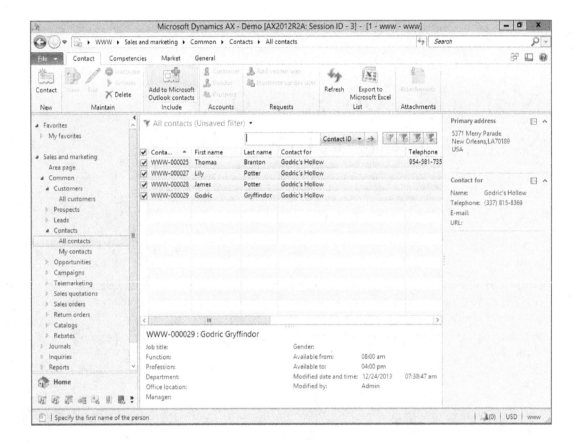

Open up the **Contacts** list page, select the contacts that you want to synchronize with Outlook, and then click the **Add to Microsoft Outlook contacts** button within the **Include** group of the **Contacts** ribbon bar.

Marking Contacts To Synchronize With Outlook

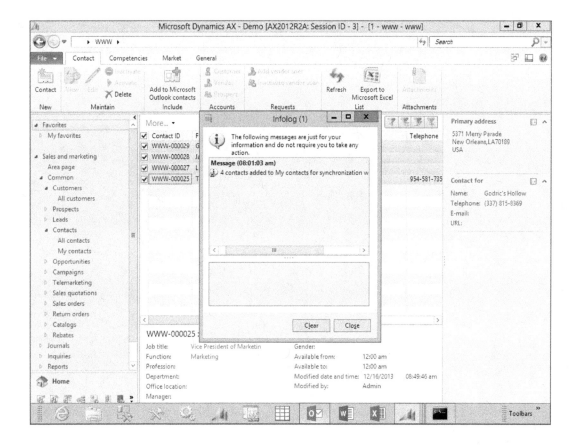

You will probably get an Infolog box telling you that the contacts have been added to the synchronization group, which you can just click the **Close** button to finish the process.

Linking To Outlook For Synchronization

Once you have marked your contacts for synchronization, you need to link your Dynamics AX user with Microsoft Outlook in order to allow you to perform the synchronization process. Luckily it's not a tricky process.

In this section we will show you how to run the **Microsoft Outlook setup wizard** to link Dynamics AX and Outlook.

Linking To Outlook For Synchronization

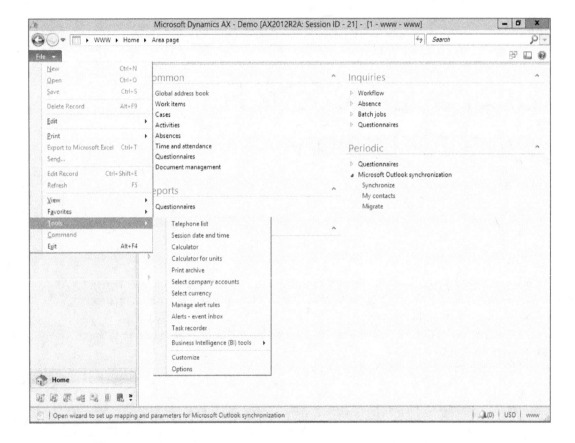

Before we start, there is one quick check that we need to make before we can start the linking process. So from the **Files** menu, select the **Tools** and then the **Options** submenu.

Linking To Outlook For Synchronization

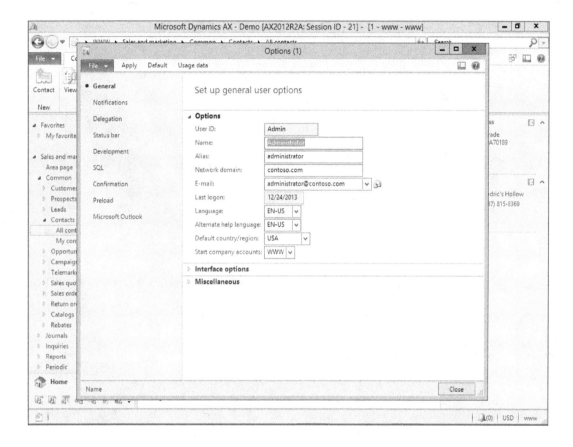

When the **Options** dialog box is displayed, check that the **E-mail** field has the same e-mail address that you are using for Outlook. After this check, just click on the **Close** button to return back to the main client.

Linking To Outlook For Synchronization

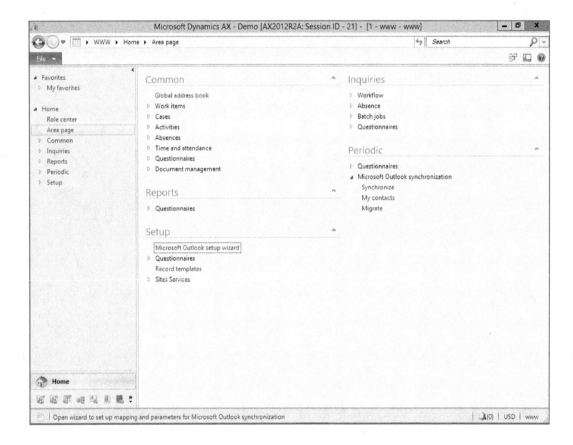

Now click on the **Microsoft Outlook setup wizard** menu item within the **Setup** group of the **Home** area page.

Linking To Outlook For Synchronization

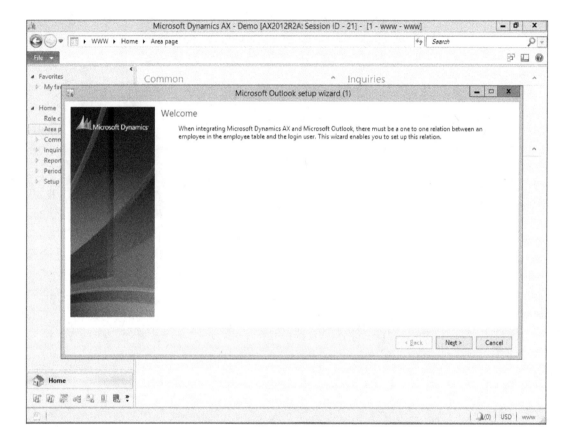

When the wizard appears, click on the **Next** button to bypass the welcome screen.

Linking To Outlook For Synchronization

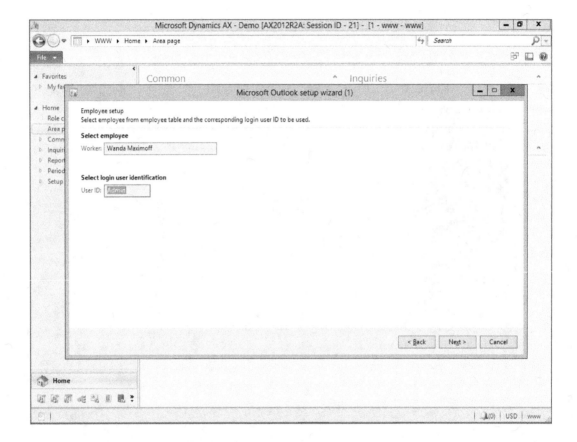

On the **Employee Setup** page, your e-mail account should automatically populate from your login information, and you can click on the **Next** button to continue on.

Linking To Outlook For Synchronization

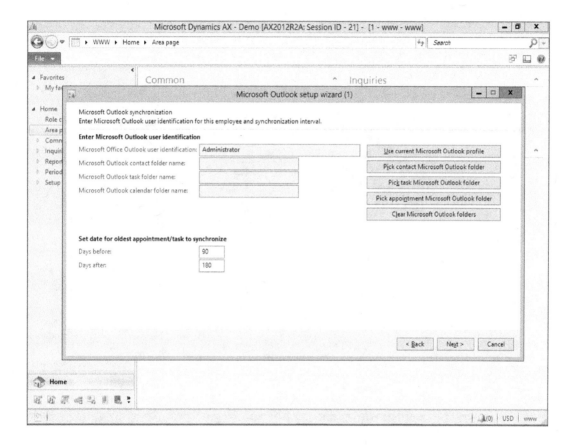

When the **Microsoft Outlook synchronization** page is displayed, check that the **Microsoft Office Outlook user identification** field is populated. If it is not then click on the **Use current Microsoft Outlook profile** button to link your profile.

Then click on the **Pick contact Microsoft Outlook folder** menu button.

Linking To Outlook For Synchronization

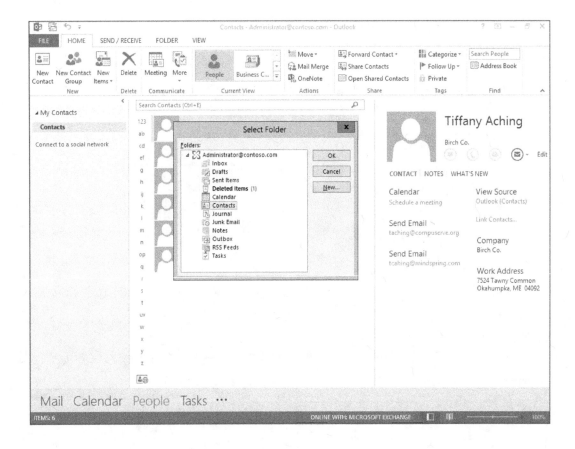

This will open up a folder chooser from Microsoft Outlook where you can select the folder that you want to synchronize the contacts from Dynamics AX to, and then click the **OK** button.

Linking To Outlook For Synchronization

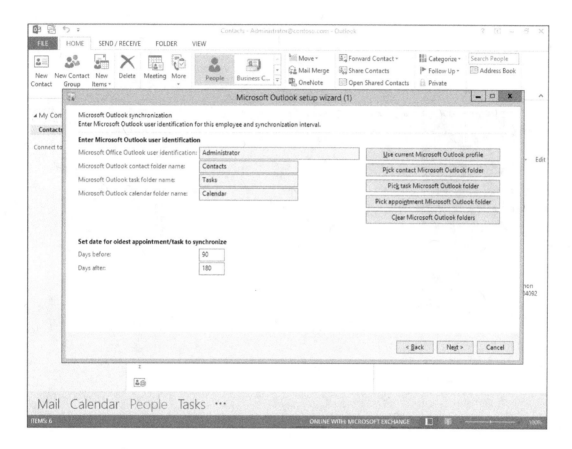

Repeat this process by clicking on the **Pick task Microsoft Outlook folder** button, and then the **Pick appointment Microsoft Outlook folder**.

If you want to override the date ranges for the synchronization then you can, and when you have finished, click on the **Next** button.

Linking To Outlook For Synchronization

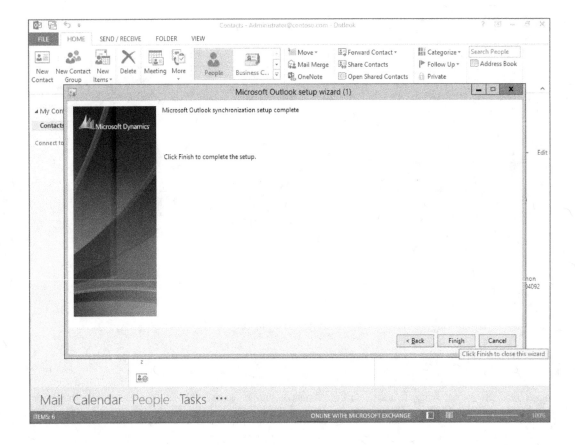

To finish the process, all you need to do is click the **Finish** button on the final page of the wizard.

Synchronizing Contacts With Outlook

Once the Synchronization is configured, it's just a matter of running the synchronization task within Dynamics AX.

In this section we will show you how to run the Synchronization process within Dynamics AX.

Synchronizing Contacts With Outlook

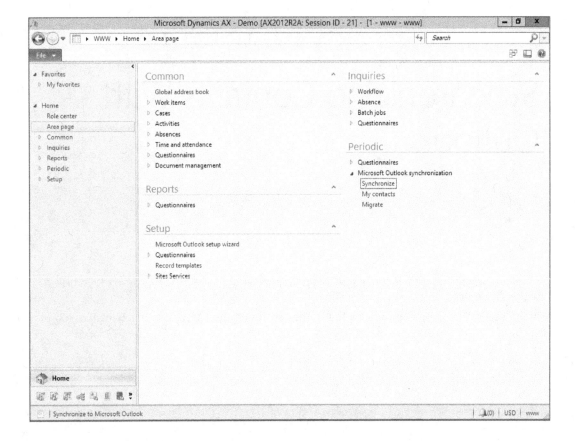

To Synchronize Dynamics AX and Outlook, click on the **Synchronize** menu item within the **Microsoft Outlook Synchronization** folder of the **Periodic** group of the **Home** area page.

Synchronizing Contacts With Outlook

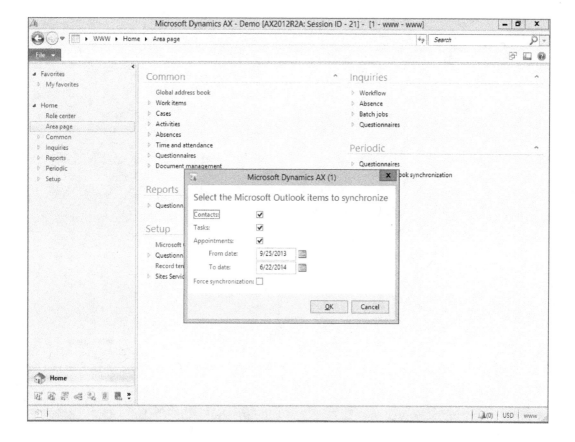

When the Synchronization dialog box is displayed, select the elements that you want to synchronize and then click the **OK** button.

Synchronizing Contacts With Outlook

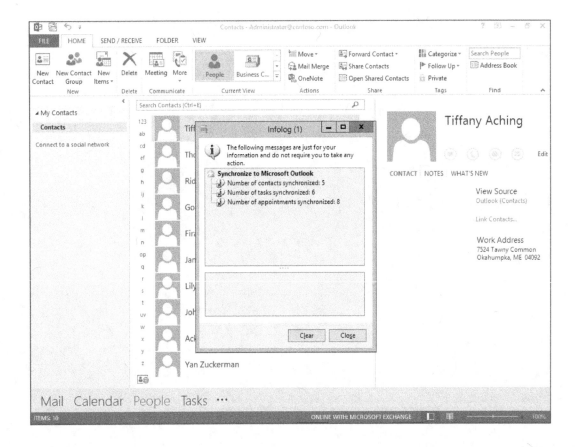

If everything is configured correctly, you will get and Infolog message telling you that you have successfully synchronized with Outlook and also how many records were synchronized.

Synchronizing Contacts With Outlook

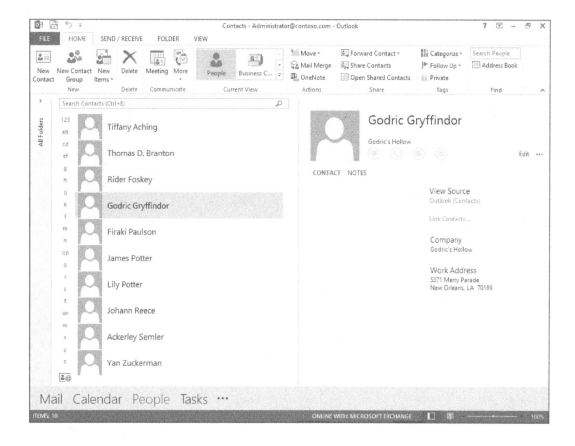

If you open up Outlook, you will now see all of the contacts that were in Dynamics AX are also available within Outlook.

CONFIGURING PROSPECT MANAGEMENT

The Sales and Marketing module within Dynamics AX does a lot more than just track the customers and contacts. You can also configure it to track prospective customers as well by configuring the prospect management features. By using **Prospects**, you can reduce the clutter within the customer master because you can track all of the information about the prospect separately, and then only convert them to a customer when you are about to do business with them. The added benefit of this is that all of the history around the prospect transfers over to the customer record, so you never loose track of anything that you did with them.

Additionally, you can use the Prospect management to track other people or organizations that you may be in contact with such as third parties to customers, and social media contacts, because they cam just be different types of prospect relations within the system. That means that you can track activities against them even if they are never going to become a customer.

In this chapter we will show how you can configure the Prospect Management within Dynamics AX to get even more out of the system.

Defining Prospect Relation Types

Before we start creating **Prospects** in the system, we need to define at least one **Prospect Relation Type**. This a a way that we can classify Prospects into different groups, and also identify key prospects later on for Lead Management.

In this example we will show how you can define the **Prospect Relation Types.**

Defining Prospect Relation Types

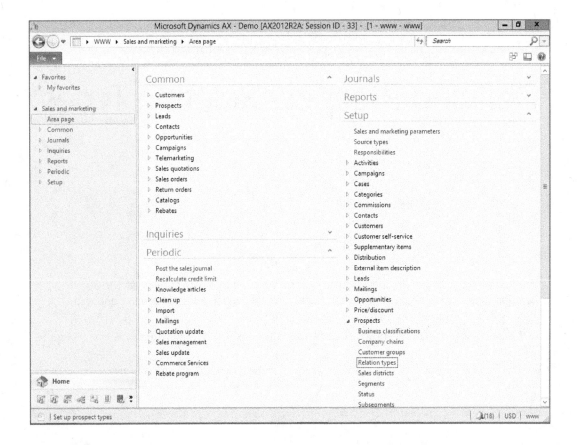

Select the **Relation Types** menu item from within the **Prospects** folder of the **Setup** group of the **Sales and Marketing** area page.

Defining Prospect Relation Types

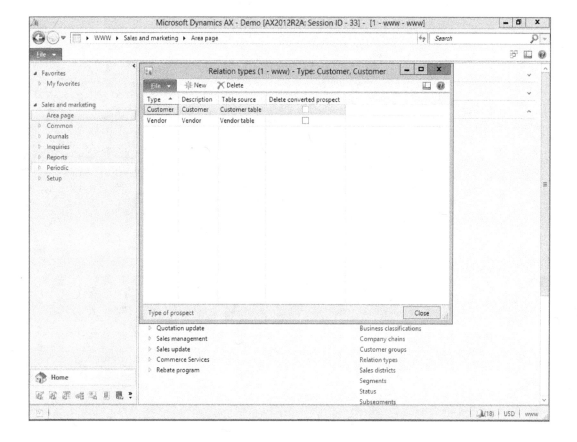

When the **Relation types** maintenance form is displayed, click on the **New** button in the menu bar to add a new record.

Defining Prospect Relation Types

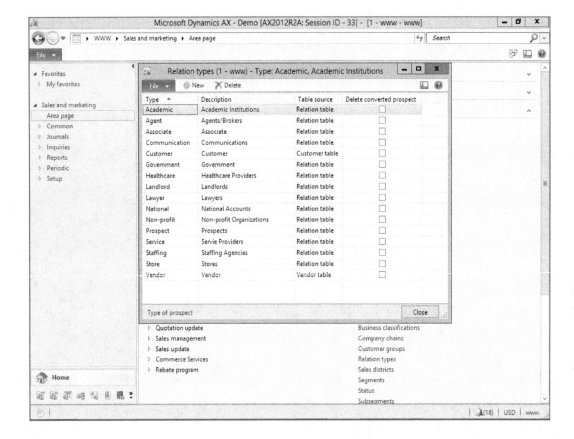

When you have finished setting up your **Relation types** click on the **Close** button to exit the form.

Defining Prospect Segmentation

We can also further categorize our Prospects by defining **Prospect Segmentation** within Dynamics AX. The segmentation is another tool that we can use later on to select prospects when we create target lists for campaigns and call lists.

In this example we will show how you can configure the **Prospect Segmentation.**

Defining Prospect Segmentation

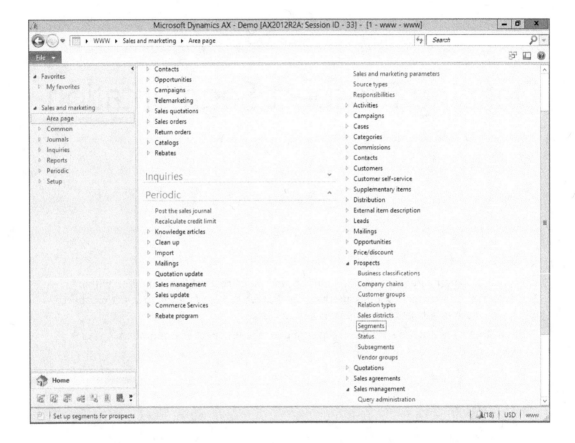

Select the **Segments** menu item from within the **Prospects** folder of the **Setup** group of the **Sales and Marketing** area page.

Defining Prospect Segmentation

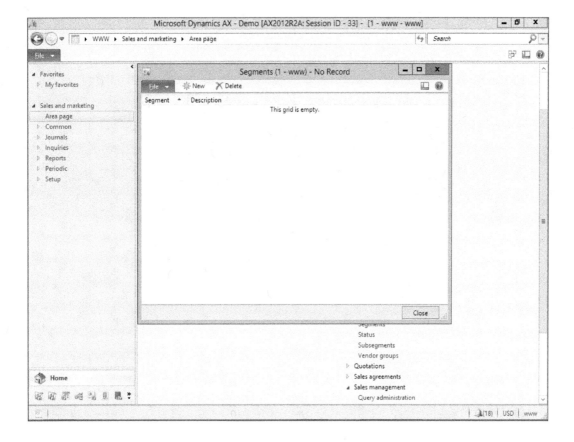

When the **Segments** maintenance form is displayed, click on the **New** button in the menu bar to add a new record.

Defining Prospect Segmentation

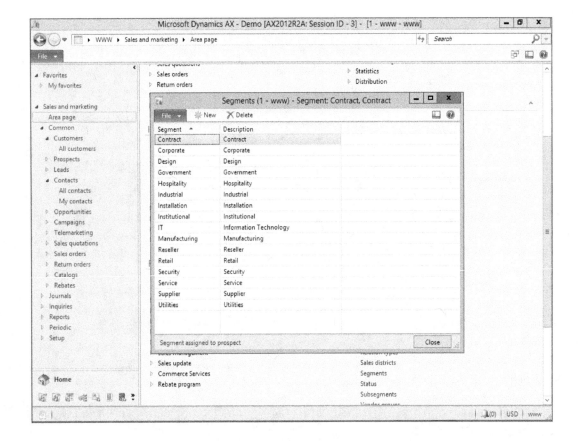

When you have finished setting up your **Segments** click on the **Close** button to exit the form.

Defining Prospect Segmentation

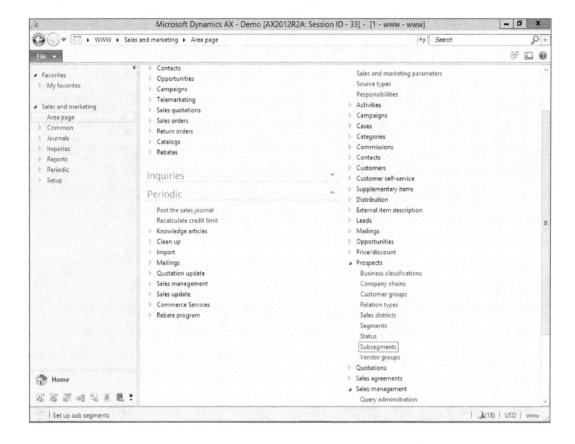

If you want to classify your prospects even more, then you can also configure the **Subsegments.** To do this, click on the **Subsegments** menu item from within the **Prospects** folder of the **Setup** group of the **Sales and Marketing** area page.

Defining Prospect Segmentation

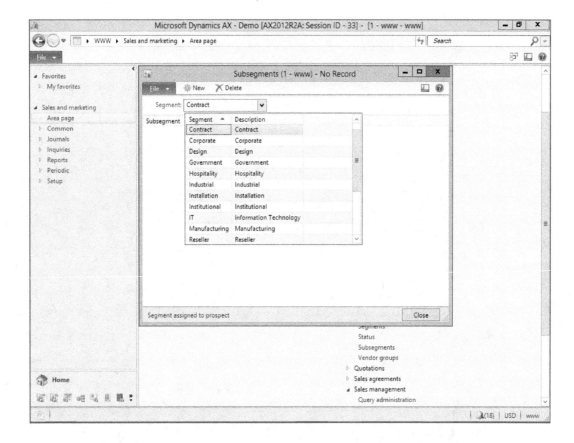

When the **Subsegments** maintenance form is displayed, select the **Segment** from the dropdown box that you want to create **Subsegments** for and click on the **New** button in the menu bar to add a new record.

Defining Prospect Segmentation

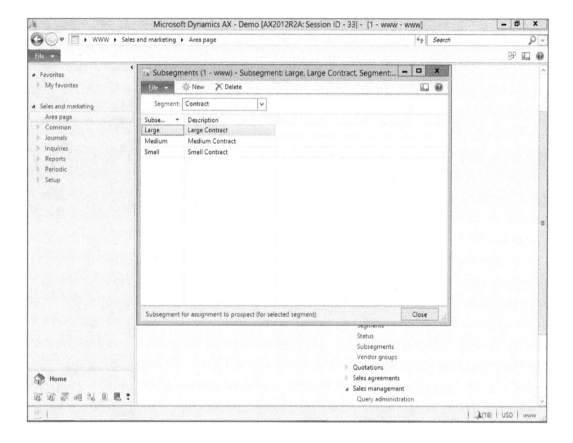

After you have finished adding all of the **Subsegments**, click on the close button to exit the maintenance form.

Defining Prospect Statuses

You can also define **Statuses** for the prospects within Dynamics AX so that you are able to see which are hot, and which are not so hot during the sales cycles.

In this example we will show how you can configure **Statuses** for Prospects.

Defining Prospect Statuses

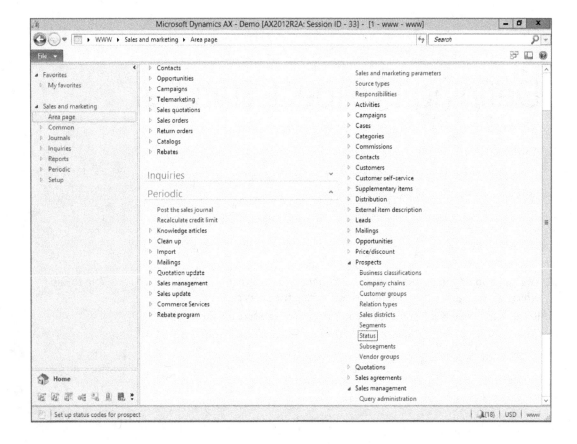

Select the **Status** menu item from within the **Prospects** folder of the **Setup** group of the **Sales and Marketing** area page.

Defining Prospect Statuses

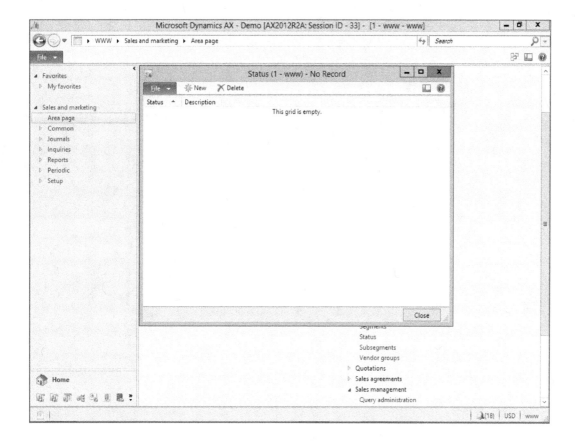

When the **Status** maintenance form is displayed, click on the **New** button in the menu bar to add a new record.

Defining Prospect Statuses

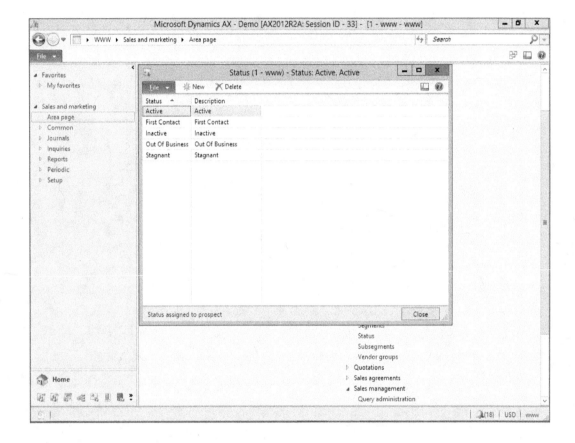

When you have finished setting up your **Statuses** click on the **Close** button to exit the form.

Defining Sales Districts

Another way that you can segregate out your **Prospects** is through **Sales Districts** You can use these to create regional categorizations for the **Prospects** that you then use when assigning your sales team to them.

In this example we will show how you can define a set of **Sales Districts**.

Defining Sales Districts

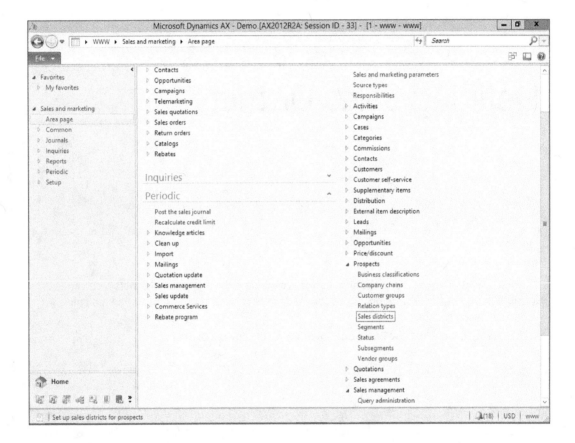

Select the **Sales Districts** menu item from within the **Prospects** folder of the **Setup** group of the **Sales and Marketing** area page.

Defining Sales Districts

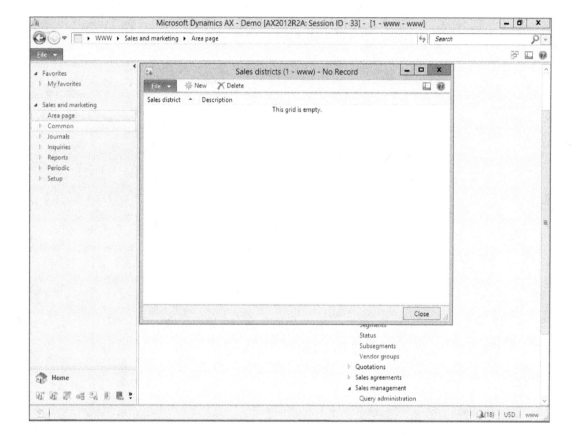

When the **Sales District** maintenance form is displayed, click on the **New** button in the menu bar to add a new record.

Defining Sales Districts

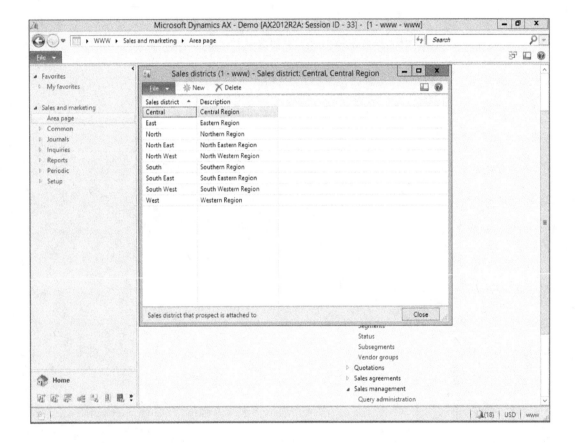

When you have finished setting up your **Sales Districts** click on the **Close** button to exit the form.

Creating New Prospects

Once you have defined the ways that you want to classify and manage your **Prospects** you can start creating them within **Dynamics AX**.

In this example we will show how you can create a new **Prospect.**

Creating New Prospects

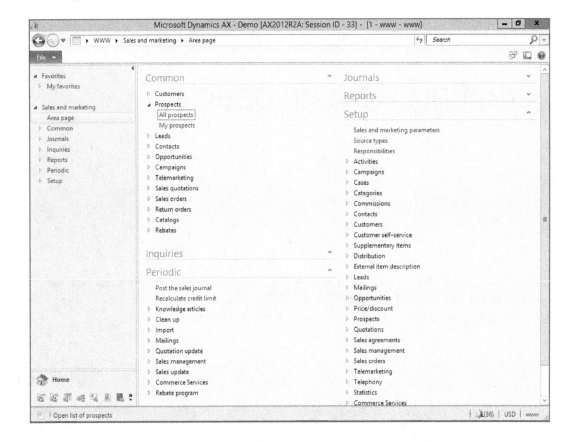

Select the **All Prospects** menu item from within the **Prospects** folder of the **Common** group of the **Sales and Marketing** area page.

Creating New Prospects

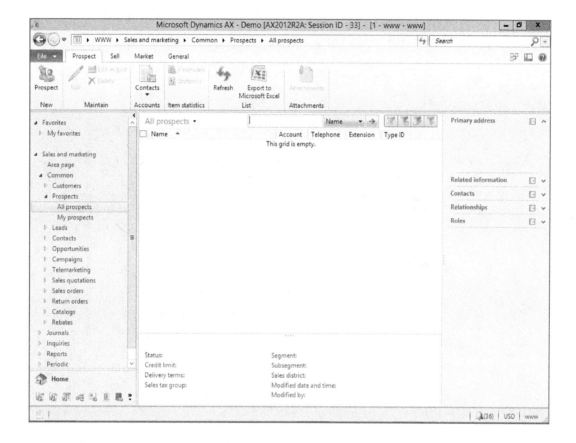

When the **All Prospects** explorer is displayed, click on the **Prospect** button within the **New** group of the **Prospect** ribbon bar.

Creating New Prospects

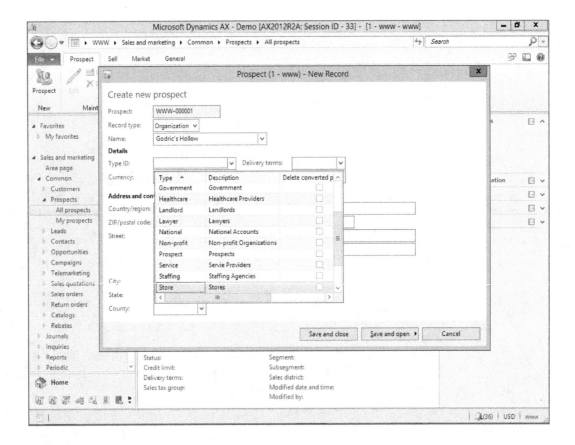

When the **Prospect** quick entry form is displayed, you can give your prospect a **Name**, and also a **Relation Type**.

Creating New Prospects

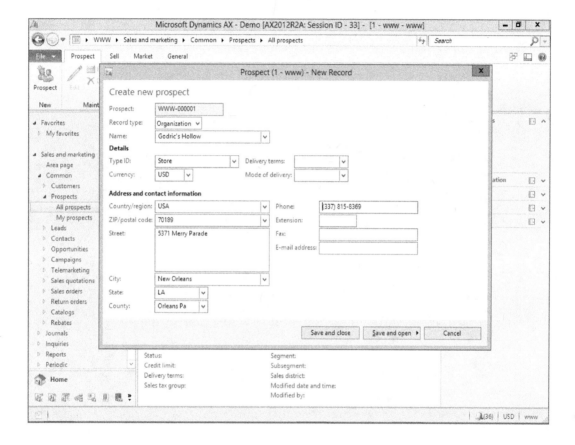

Then all you need to do is fill in the address and contact information and then then click on the **Save and open** button.

Creating New Prospects

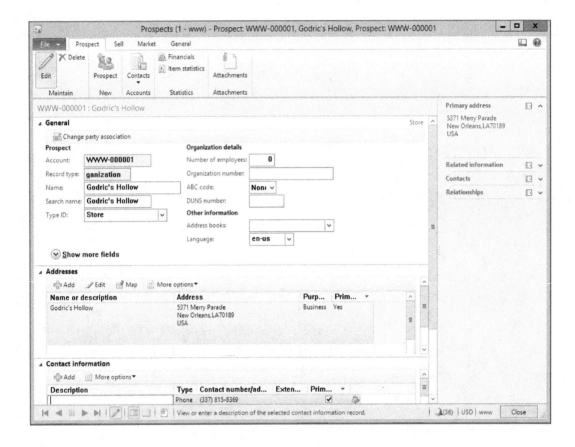

This will open up the main maintenance form for the **Prospect** with all of the core information already populated.

Creating New Prospects

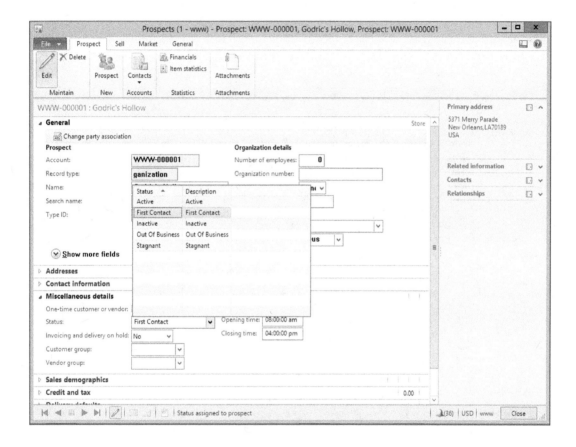

You can update the **Status** field within the **Miscellaneous details** tab of the Prospect.

Creating New Prospects

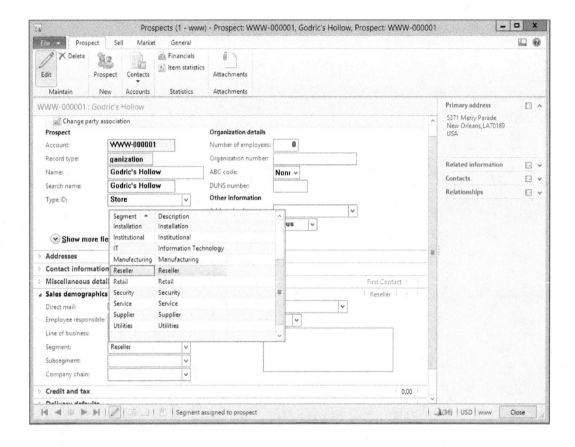

And also you can update the **Segment** and **Subsegment** for the prospect within the **Sales demographics** tab.

When you are done, you can click the **Close** button to exit the form.

Creating Contacts for Prospects

Prospects are just a precursor to a Customer, and as a result, you can track all of the same contact information against it that you can against a Customer. When the Prospect gets converted over to a Customer, then all of this contact information will be associated with the Customer as well, saving a lot of double entry.

In this example we will show how you can create **Contacts** for **Prospects.**

Creating Contacts for Prospects

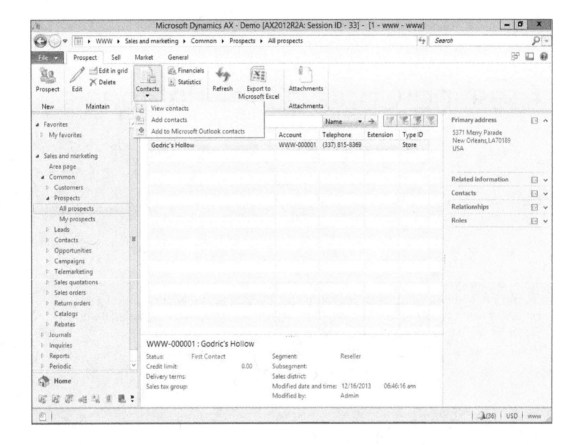

From either the Prospect list or detail page, select the **Add contact** submenu item from the **Contacts** menu button within the **Accounts** group of the **Prospects** ribbon bar.

Creating Contacts for Prospects

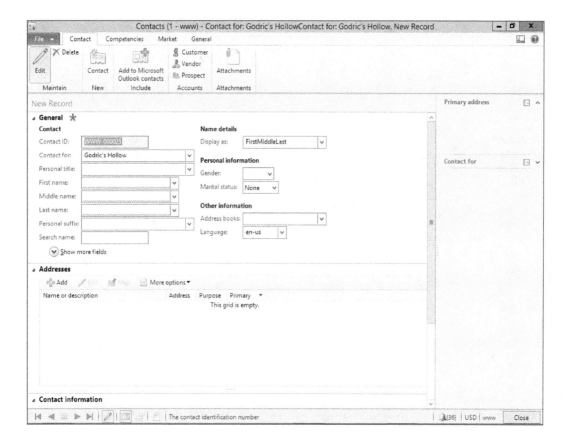

When the new **Contact** form is displayed, it will already be linked to the Prospect through the **Contact for** field.

Creating Contacts for Prospects

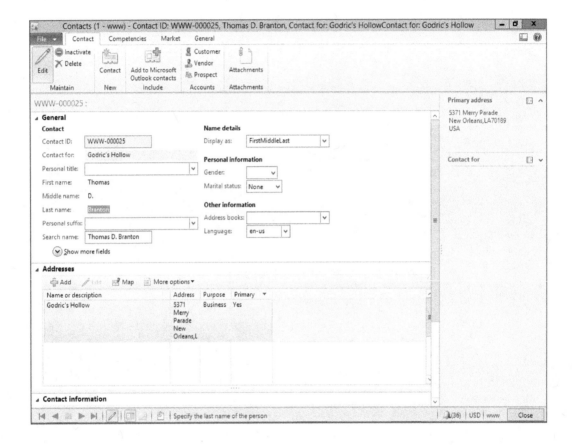

As soon as you enter in the name and save the record, all of the address information will copy over to the Contact record from the Prospect.

Creating Contacts for Prospects

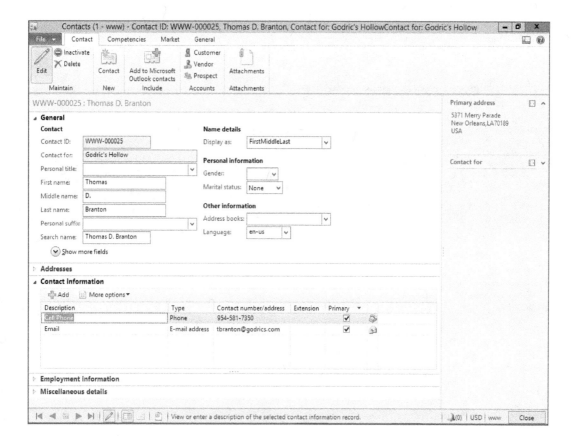

You can also add additional details within the **Contact information** tab.

Creating Contacts for Prospects

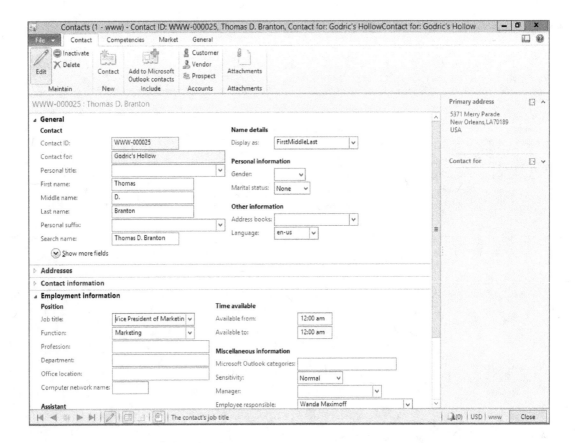

And you can update any of the professional information within the **Employment Information** tab.

When you have updated the Contact, you can just click on the **Close** button to return back to the main menu.

Converting a Prospect Into a Customer

Whenever you want to, you can convert a **Prospect** into a **Customer** with just a couple of mouse-clicks. This will allow you then to start selling to them, which is what you really the end goal anyway.

In this example we will show how to convert a **Prospect** into a **Customer**.

Converting a Prospect Into a Customer

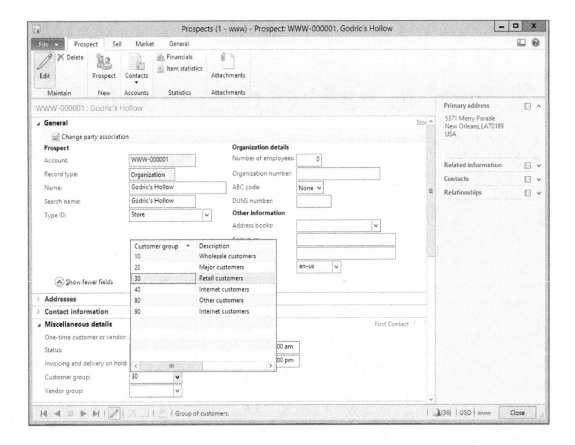

Before we start, we need to make sure that the **Customer Group** fields is populated on the **Prospect** record. This is a required field for Customers, and if we try the conversion with this field being blank, then Dynamics AX will complain a little.

Converting a Prospect Into a Customer

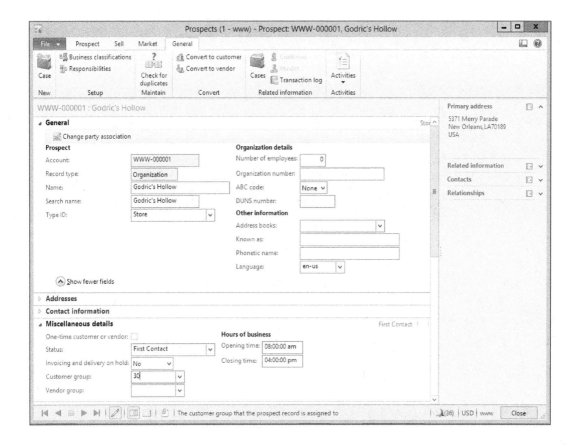

To covert a **Prospect** into a **Customer**, just open up the **Prospect** record, and click on the **Convert to Customer** menu button within the **Convert** group of the **General** ribbon bar.

Converting a Prospect Into a Customer

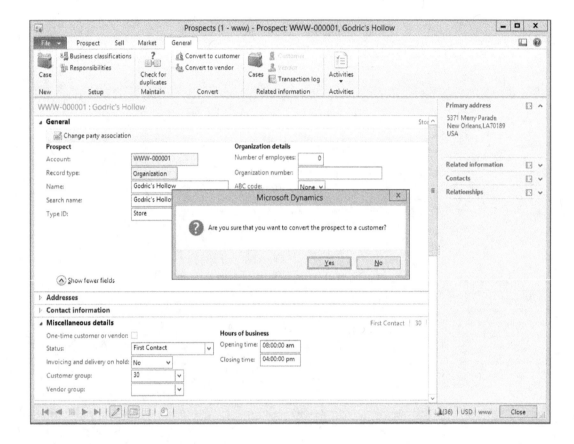

When the confirmation dialog box is displayed, just click on the **Yes** button to start the process.

Converting a Prospect Into a Customer

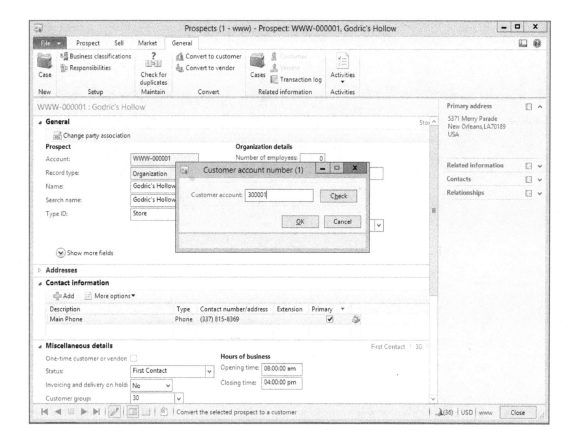

If you have manual customer numbering turned on them you will be asked to type in the number that you want to assign to the new **Customer.**

Converting a Prospect Into a Customer

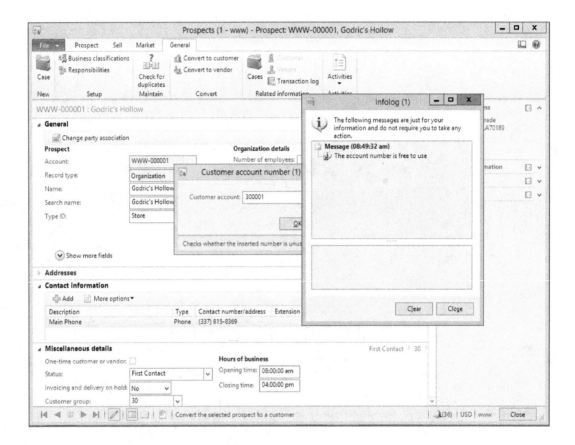

It may be a good idea to click on the **Check** menu button, then it will make sure that the Customer Number is not already in use.

Converting a Prospect Into a Customer

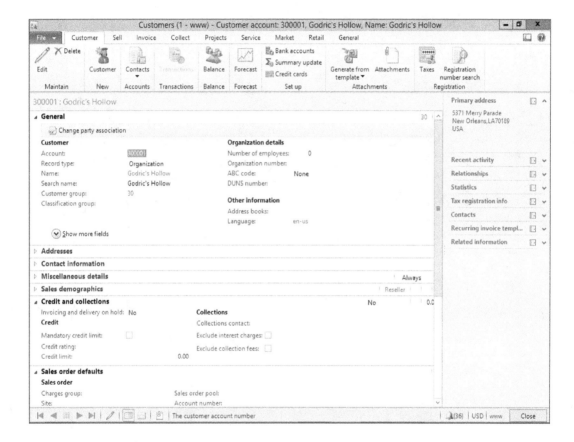

After clicking on the **OK** button, all of the information from the **Prospect** will be converted over into a **Customer** record for you.

How easy was that.

Converting a Prospect Into a Customer

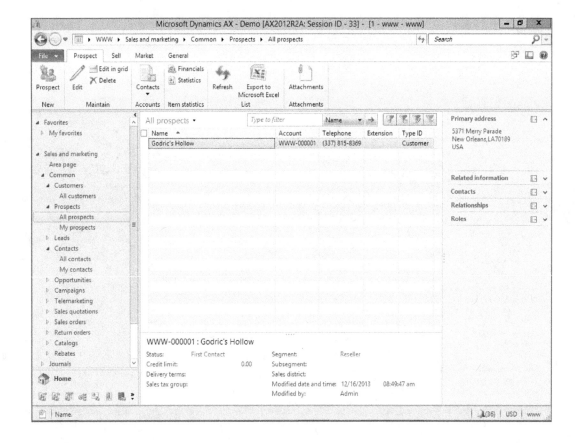

Also, if you return to your **Prospects** list page, and if you did not check the **Delete converted prospect** option within the **Prospect Relations** your prospect record will now have a Type ID of **Customer** which identifies that it was converted into a Customer record.

CONFIGURING OPPORTUNITY MANAGEMENT

Once you are tracking Prospects within Dynamics AX, the next area that you should look at configuring is the **Opportunity Management**. This will allow you to create **Opportunity** records, track the **Competition** and also create **Quotations** that you can then convert automatically into **Sales Orders** without having to rekey in any additional information.

In this chapter we will show how you can easily configure the **Opportunity Management** features of Dynamics AX.

Defining Opportunity Phases

We can define **Phases** for **Opportunities** so that we can track the general state of our **Opportunities**. This is useful for reporting and analysis later on.

In this example we will show how to define **Opportunity Phases**.

Defining Opportunity Phases

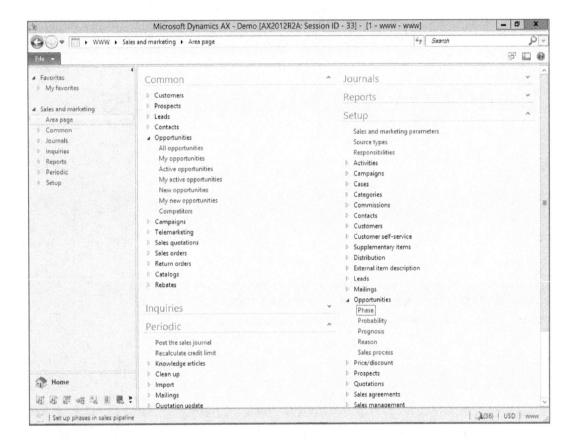

Select the **Phase** menu item from within the **Opportunities** folder of the **Setup** group of the **Sales and Marketing** area page.

Defining Opportunity Phases

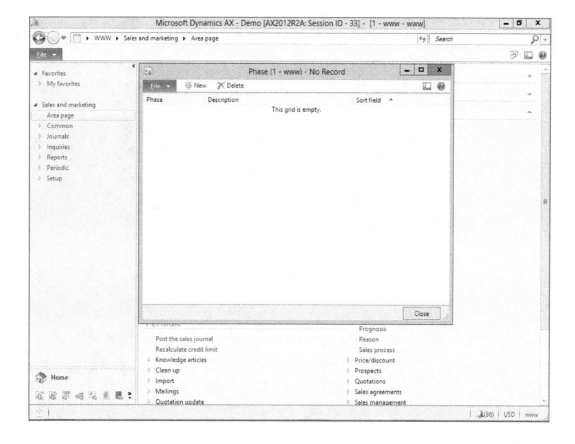

When the **Phases** maintenance form is displayed, click on the **New** button in the menu bar to add a new record.

Defining Opportunity Phases

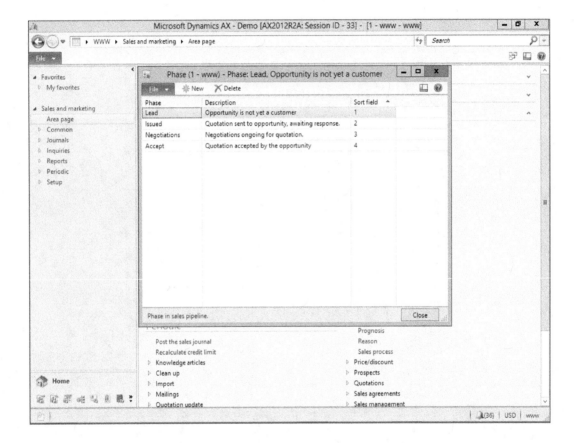

When you have finished setting up your **Phases** click on the **Close** button to exit the form.

Defining Opportunity Probability

Another way to track the status of the **Opportunities** is to define the probability to close for an **Opportunity** based on the phase or stage that it is in. We can do this by creating **Probability** levels.

In this example we will show how to set up **Probability** levels.

Defining Opportunity Probability

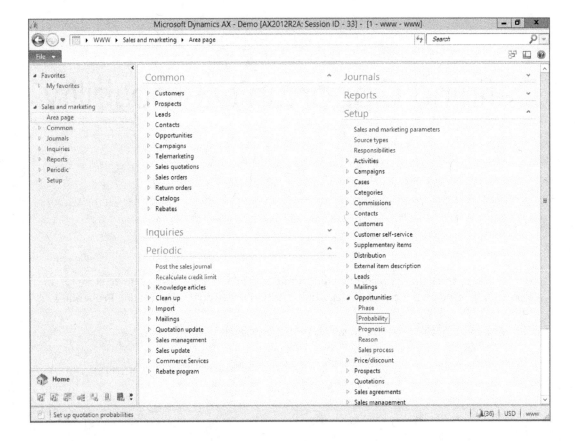

Select the **Probability** menu item from within the **Opportunities** folder of the **Setup** group of the **Sales and Marketing** area page.

Defining Opportunity Probability

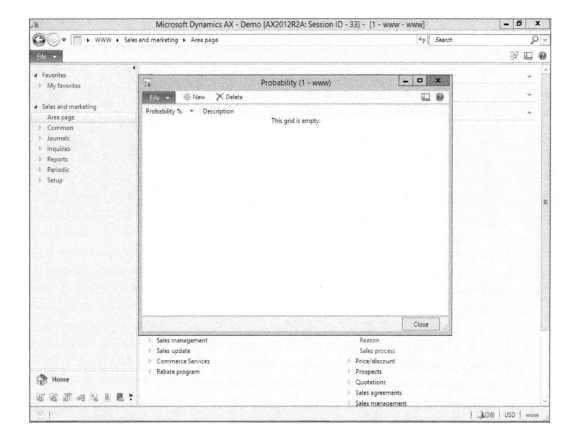

When the **Probability** maintenance form is displayed, click on the **New** button in the menu bar to add a new record.

Defining Opportunity Probability

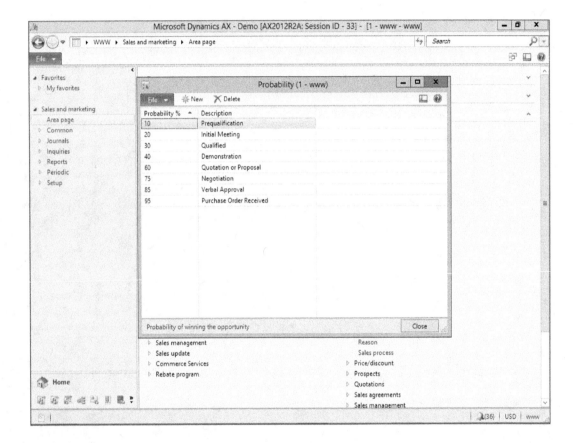

When you have finished setting up your **Probability** click on the **Close** button to exit the form.

Defining Opportunity Prognosis

Another way that you can classify **Opportunities** is by assigning them a **Prognosis**. This is a way that you can estimate the closing time frame, and this may then be used later on in your sales reporting.

In this example we will show how to define your **Opportunity Prognosis** levels.

Defining Opportunity Prognosis

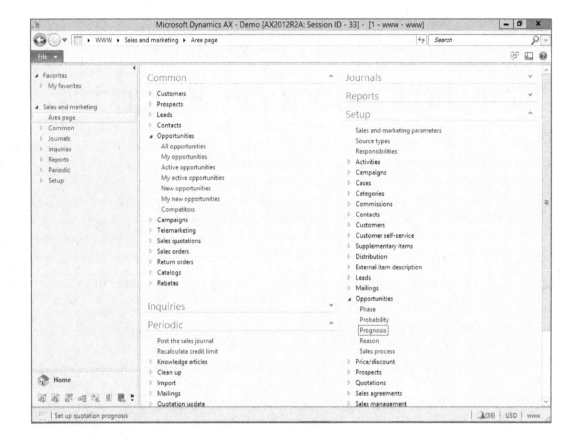

Select the **Prognosis** menu item from within the **Opportunities** folder of the **Setup** group of the **Sales and Marketing** area page.

Defining Opportunity Prognosis

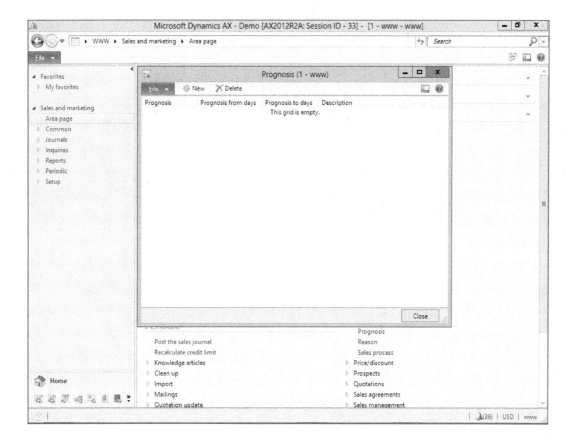

When the **Prognosis** maintenance form is displayed, click on the **New** button in the menu bar to add a new record.

Defining Opportunity Prognosis

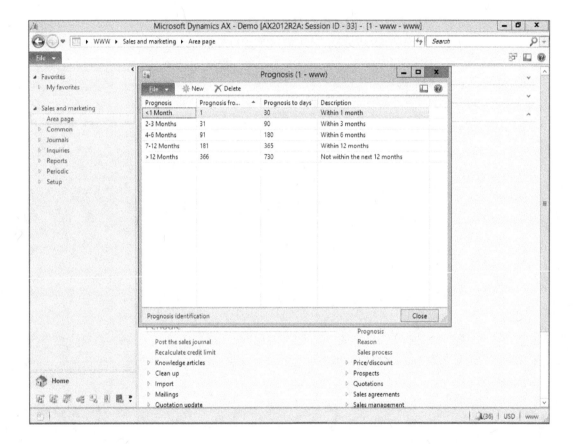

When you have finished setting up your **Prognosis** click on the **Close** button to exit the form.

Defining Opportunity Reasons

Although all **Opportunities** are supposed to close, that is not always the case. So to track lost **Opportunities** we will need to configure the **Reasons** table that contains all of the explanations for the won or lost opportunities.

In this example we will show how to define all of the **Opportunity Reasons**.

Defining Opportunity Reasons

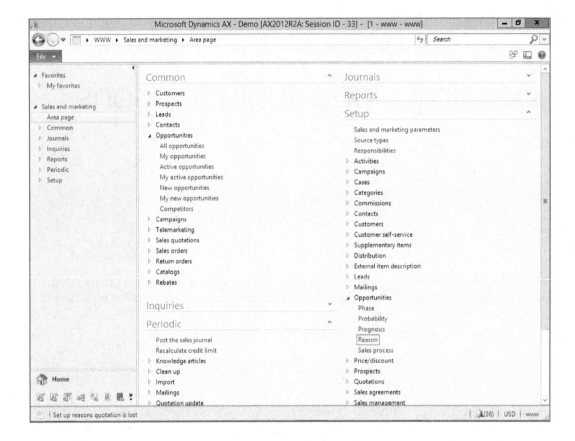

Select the **Reason** menu item from within the **Opportunities** folder of the **Setup** group of the **Sales and Marketing** area page.

Defining Opportunity Reasons

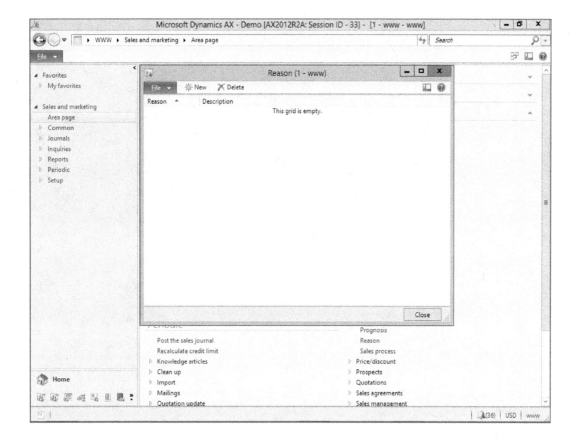

When the **Reason** maintenance form is displayed, click on the **New** button in the menu bar to add a new record.

Defining Opportunity Reasons

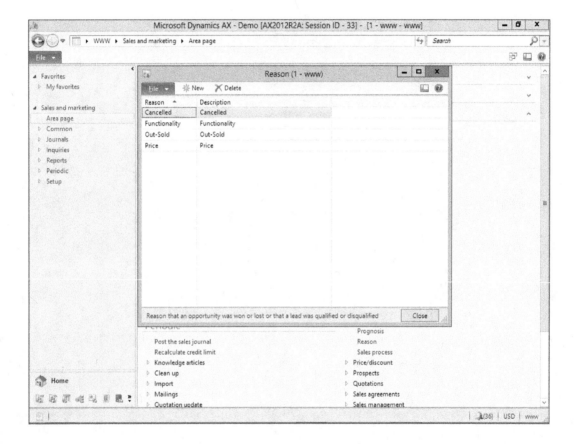

When you have finished setting up your **Reasons** click on the **Close** button to exit the form.

Configuring Sales Processes For Opportunities

To make the sales cycle a little more structured, we can configure **Sales Processes** that we can apply to **Opportunities** that allow us to track with a little more detail all of the stages that must be performed to ensure the highest probability of close. If you are already using a formal sales methodology, then this will probably be a must have for you.

In this example we will show how to define a **Sales Process** for **Opportunity** management.

Configuring Sales Processes For Opportunities

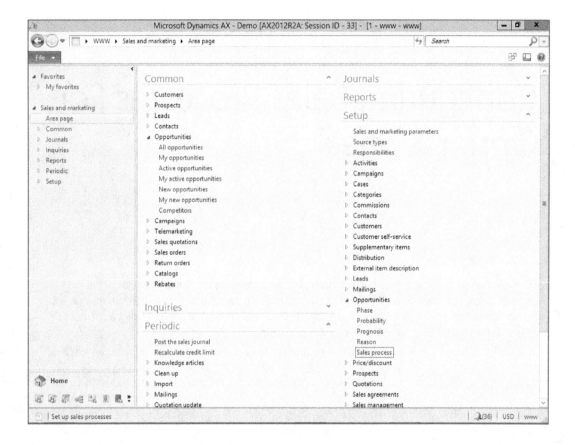

Select the **Sales Process** menu item from within the **Opportunities** folder of the **Setup** group of the **Sales and Marketing** area page.

Configuring Sales Processes For Opportunities

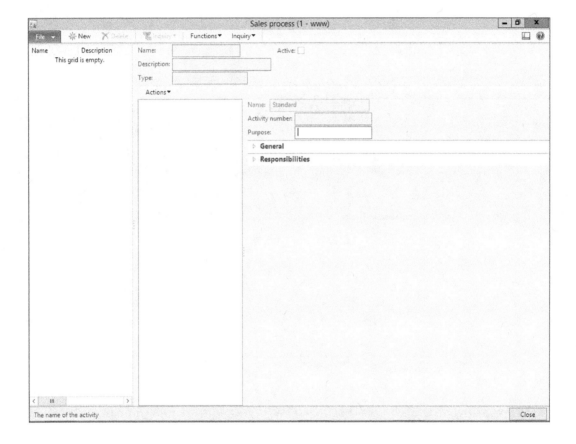

When the **Sales process** designer is displayed, click on the **New** button in the menu bar to create a new **Sales Process.**

Configuring Sales Processes For Opportunities

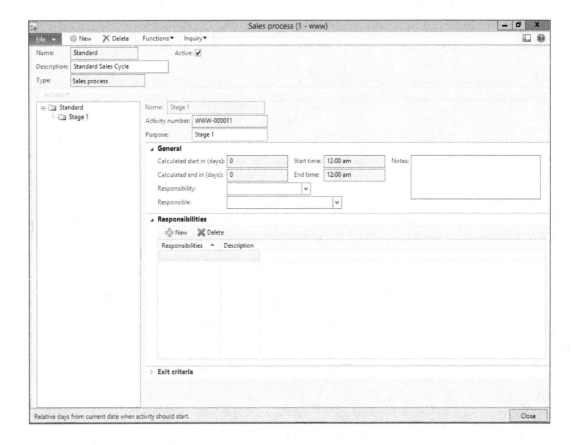

Give your new **Sales Process** a **Name** and **Description** and then save it. This will build the initial nodes for your sales process in the process tree to the right of the form.

Configuring Sales Processes For Opportunities

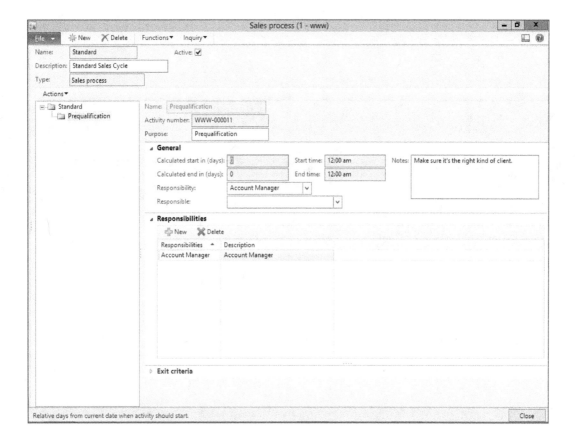

You can now give the first stage in the Sales Process a **Purpose**, assign some **Notes**, and if this is usually assigned to a particular person, then you can also assign it to a **Responsibility** type, or even a particular person in the organization by populating the **Responsible** field.

Configuring Sales Processes For Opportunities

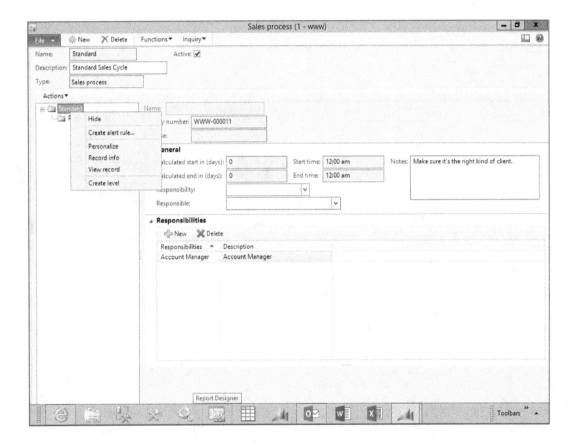

To add subsequent levels, just right-mouse-click on the topmost node, and select the **Create level** from the submenu.

Configuring Sales Processes For Opportunities

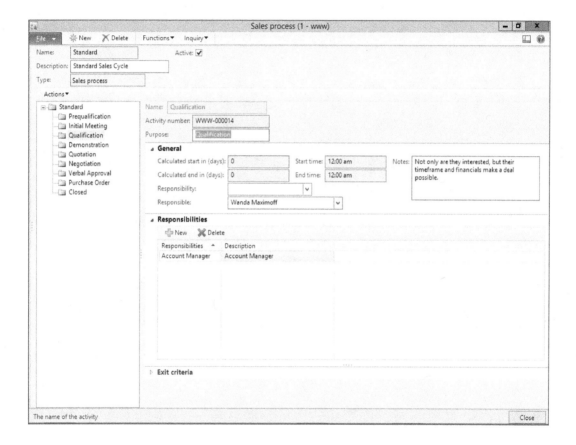

You can repeat this process until you have defined all of the steps in your sales process.

When you have finished, just click on the **Close** button.

Assigning Default Activities to Sales Processes

You can make the sales process even more automated by associating **Activities** to the nodes in the **Sales Process** tree. This will automatically create and assign activities to users when opportunities reach certain milestones.

In this example we will show how to assign default **Activities** to steps in the **Sales Processes.**

Assigning Default Activities to Sales Processes

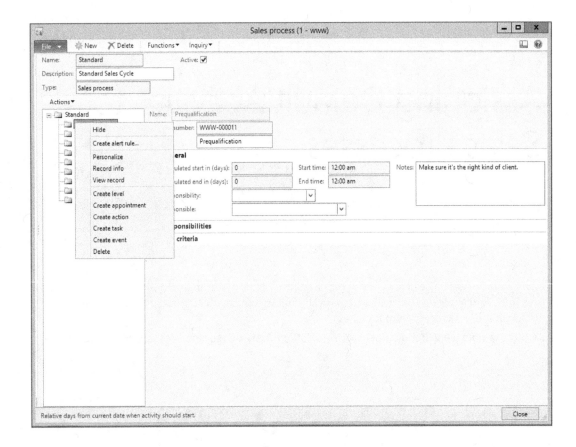

To assign an **Activity** to a step in the **Sales Process**, just right-mouse-click on the node, and then select the appropriate **Create...** submenu item.

Assigning Default Activities to Sales Processes

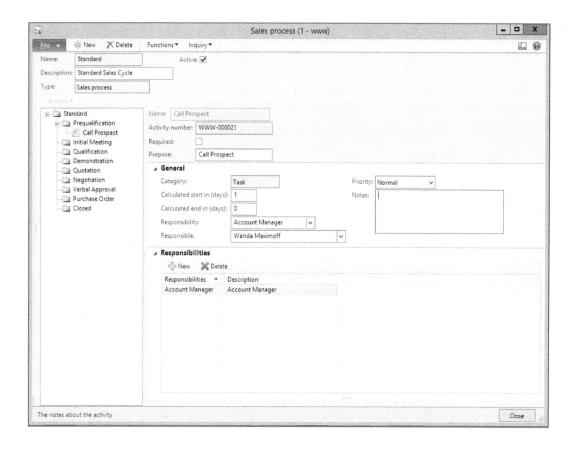

You can create **Task Activities** and assign then to particular people.

Assigning Default Activities to Sales Processes

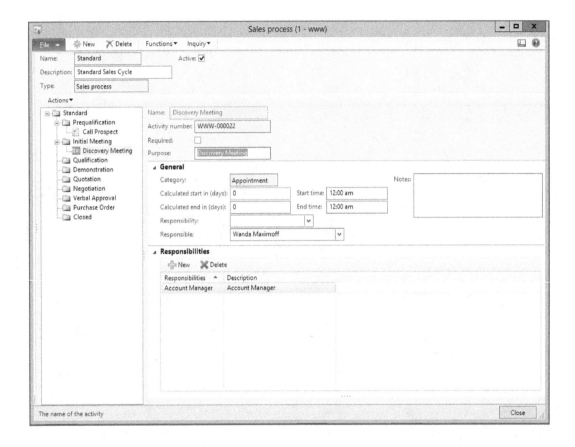

You can also create **Appointment Activities** that will automatically be created and then synchronize with Outlook.

Assigning Default Activities to Sales Processes

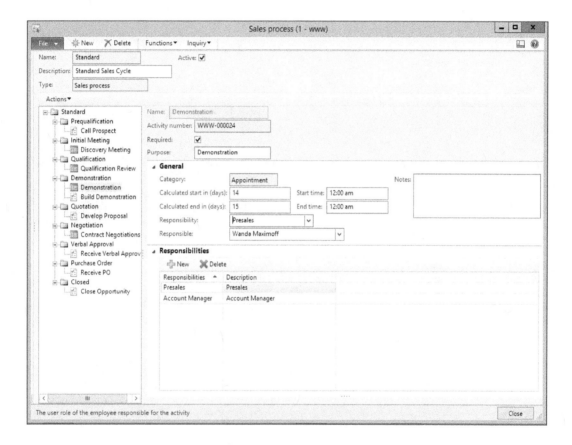

After you have assigned all of the **Activities** that you want to be created by the system, you can just click on the **Close** button to return to the main menu.

Specifying Exit Criteria For Sales Process Stages

If you want to impose even more control over the sales process, then you can also define **Exit Criteria** for any or all of the stages within the **Sales Process** that require that certain conditions have been met, and that all of the necessary information has been entered into the **Opportunity** record. This makes sure that creative users do not try to jump steps in the sales process.

In this example we will show how to configure **Exit Criteria** against stages in the **Sales Process.**

Specifying Exit Criteria For Sales Process Stages

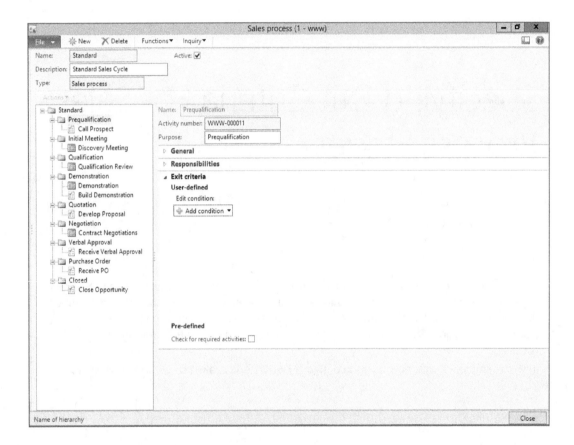

Open up the **Sales Process** that you want to control, and then select the node in the **Sales Process** that you want to control. Then open up the **Exit criteria** tab and click on the **Add condition** button.

Specifying Exit Criteria For Sales Process Stages

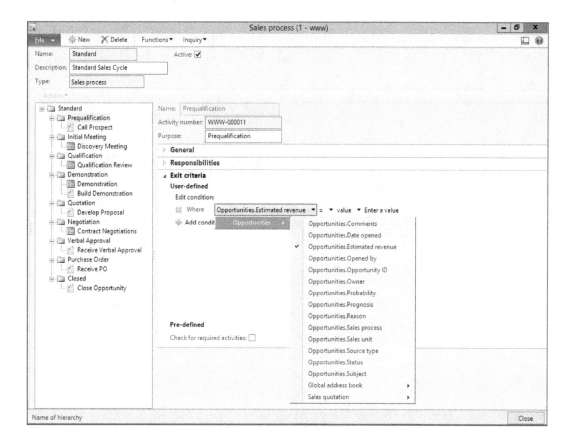

This will allow you to use any of the fields within the **Opportunity** table as criteria.

Specifying Exit Criteria For Sales Process Stages

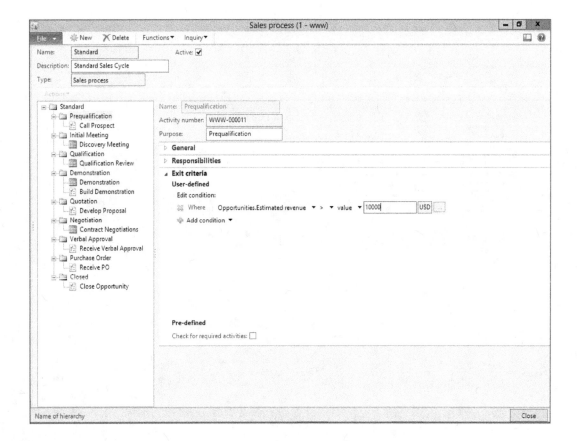

And you can also place required conditions that need to be met.

Specifying Exit Criteria For Sales Process Stages

All you have to do is continue adding conditions until you have built up your **Exit Criteria** rule.

Creating Opportunities From Prospect Records

Once we have all of our classifications and sales processes defined, we can now create opportunities. You can create **Opportunities** a number of different ways. You can create them from the **Opportunities** list page, from **Customers** and also from **Prospects**.

In this example we will show how you can create an Opportunity directly from a **Prospect** record.

Creating Opportunities From Prospect Records

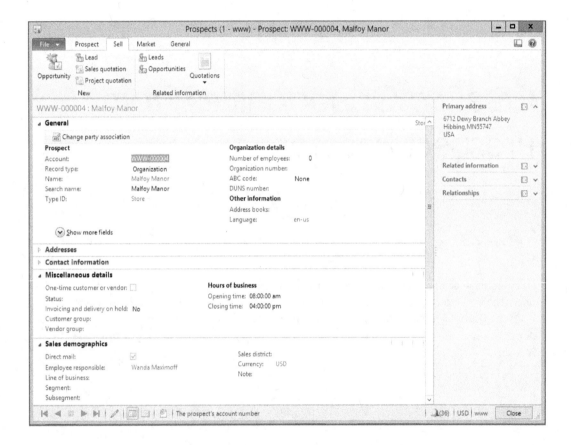

To create an **Opportunity** directly from the **Prospect** record, just click on the **Opportunity** button within the **New** group of the **Sell** ribbon bar.

Creating Opportunities From Prospect Records

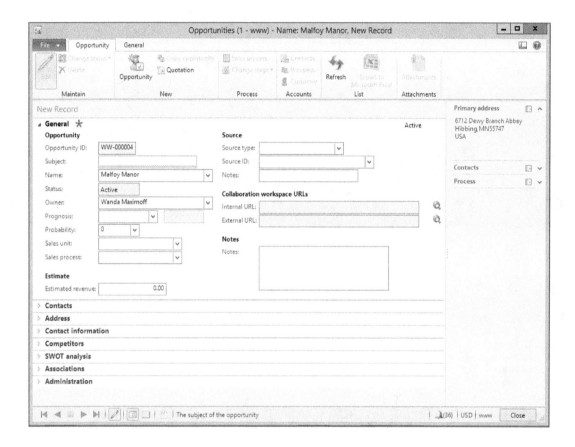

This will create a new **Opportunity** record for you.

Creating Opportunities From Prospect Records

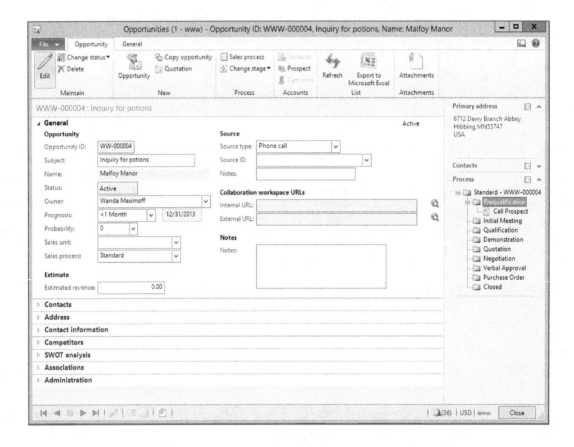

All you need to do is fill in the **Subject** and also any of the other classification fields that you may required through the sales process and click on the **Close** button.

Notice: Because we have a pre-defined **Sales Process** associated with the **Opportunity**, the process steps and current stage are shown to the right within the Fact Box panel.

Updating Sales Process Stages

If you have defined a **Sales Process** that you want to follow for all of your **Opportunities**, then you are able to change the current stage within the Opportunity itself, as long as all of the **Exit Criteria** for the stage has been satisfied.

In this example we will show how you can change the **Sales Process Stage** of an **Opportunity**.

Updating Sales Process Stages

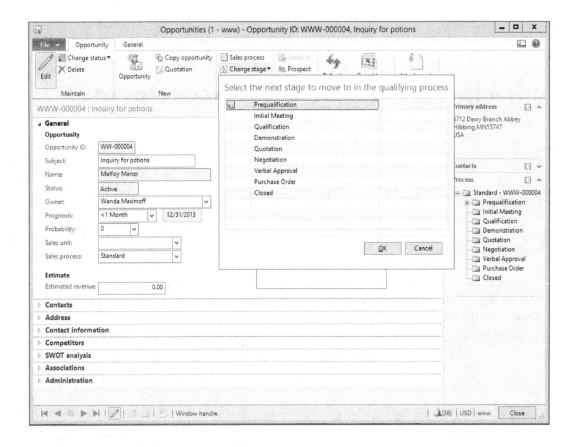

To change the **Sales Process Stage**, click on the **Change stage** menu button within the **Process** group of the **Opportunity** ribbon bar. This will show you all of the stages in the process and you just have to select the stage that you would like to move the Opportunity to.

Updating Sales Process Stages

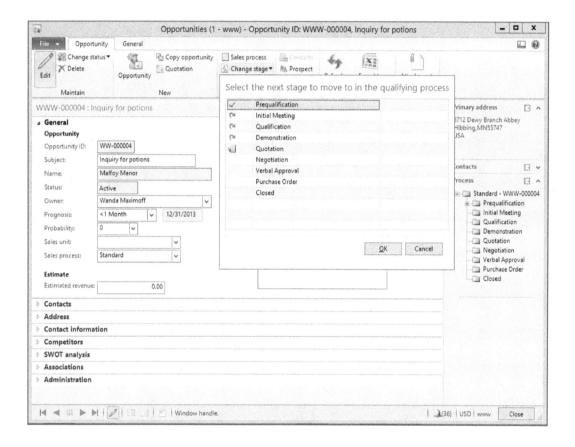

If all of the **Exit Criteria** for the stage(s) are met, then it will update for you.

Defining Competitors

When you are in a competitive situation, you may want to track who your **Competitors** are in you **Opportunities** so that you can track who you won and lost against. This is great intelligence to have especially the next time you are competing with them. The first step in this process though is to identify your competition.

In this example we will show how you can create **Competitor** records.

Defining Competitors

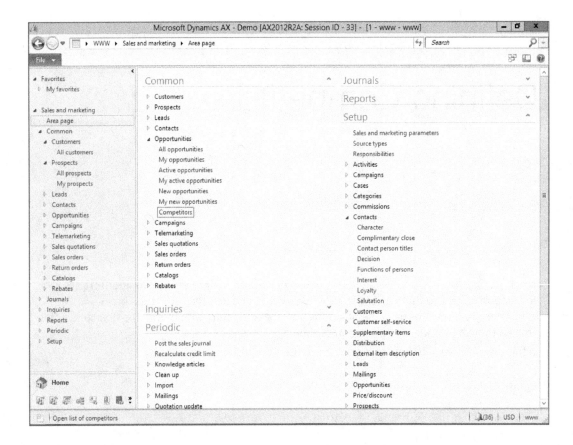

Click on the **Competitors** menu item within the **Opportunities** folder of the **Common** group of the **Sales and Marketing** area page.

Defining Competitors

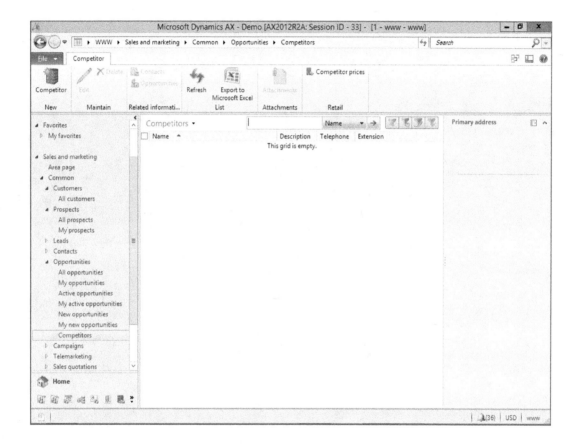

When the **Competitors** list page is displayed, click on the **Competitor** button within the **New** group of the **Competitor** ribbon bar.

Defining Competitors

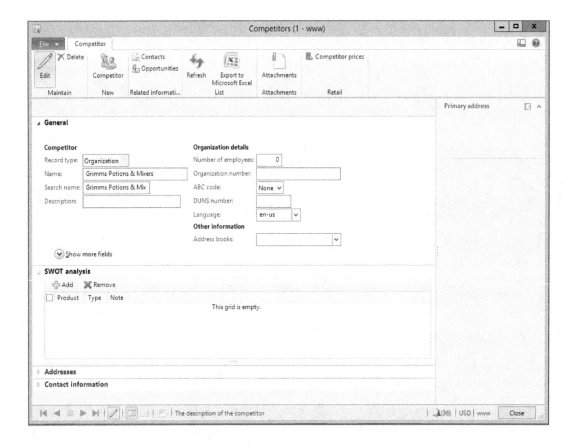

Now just give your competitor a **Name** and **Search name** and then click the **Close** button to edit the form.

Tracking Competitors Against Opportunities

Once you have defined all of your **Competitors** you then start associating them with **Opportunities** so that you can start using that information within you sales reports.

In this example we will show how you can associate **Competitors** with **Opportunities.**

Tracking Competitors Against Opportunities

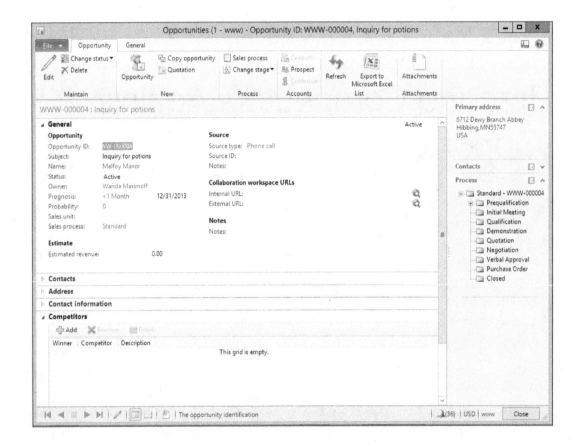

Open up your **Opportunity** record, and expand the **Competitors** tab. To associate a **Competitor** click on the **Add** button within the menu bar of the tab.

Tracking Competitors Against Opportunities

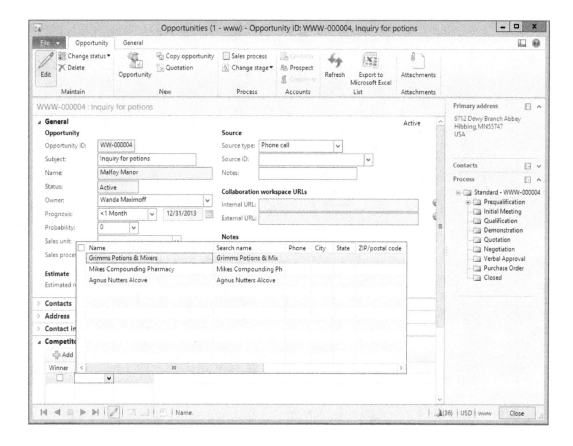

This will allow you to select the **Competitor** from the list of defined **Competition**.

Tracking Competitors Against Opportunities

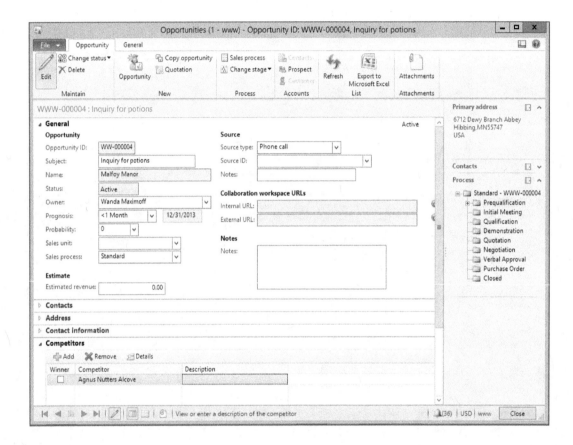

You can add as many **Competitors** as you like to an **Opportunity.**

When you are done, just click the **Close** button to exit from the form.

Creating Quotations For Opportunities

Once you have an **Opportunity** you will probably want to then create a **Quotation** against it and send it to the **Prospect**.

In this example we will show you how to create a **Quotation** directly from an **Opportunity** record.

Creating Quotations For Opportunities

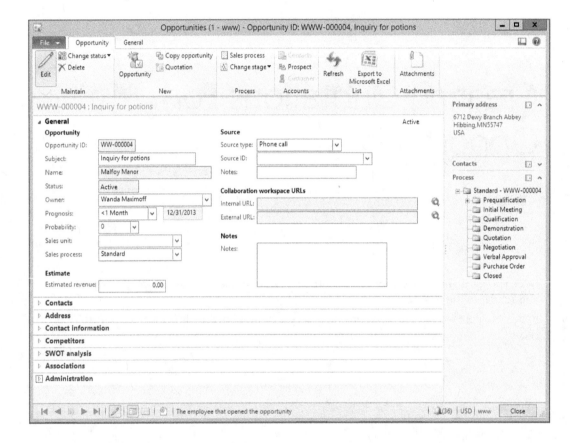

Open up the **Opportunity** that you want to create the **Quotation** for and click on the **Quotation** menu button within the **New** group of the **Opportunity** ribbon bar.

Creating Quotations For Opportunities

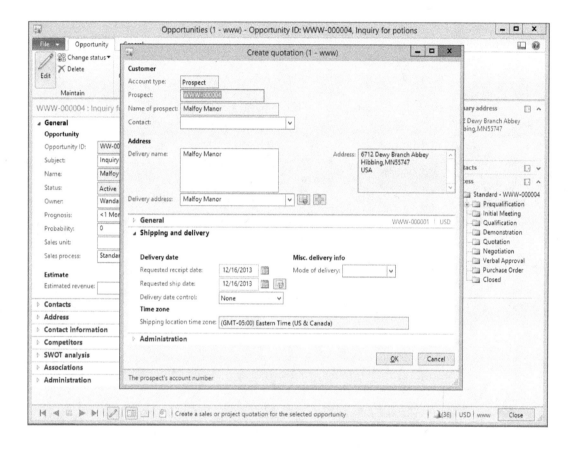

When the **Create quotation** quick entry form is displayed, you can update any of the header information, and then click on the **OK** button to create the **Quotation**.

Creating Quotations For Opportunities

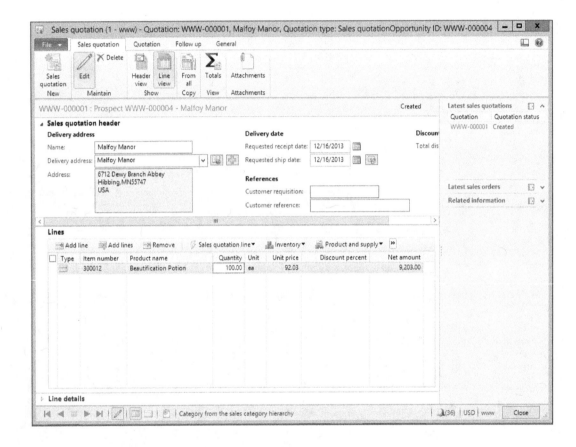

Now you just need to fill out the details for the **Quotation.**

Creating Quotations For Opportunities

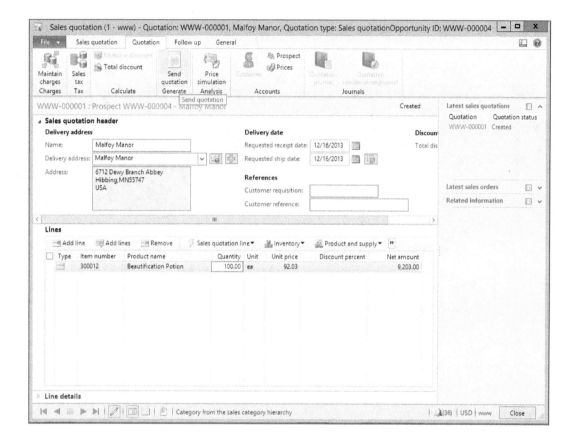

Once the **Quotation** has been completed, you can click on the **Send Quotation** button within the **Generate** group of the **Quotation** ribbon bar to send it to the **Prospect.**

Creating Quotations For Opportunities

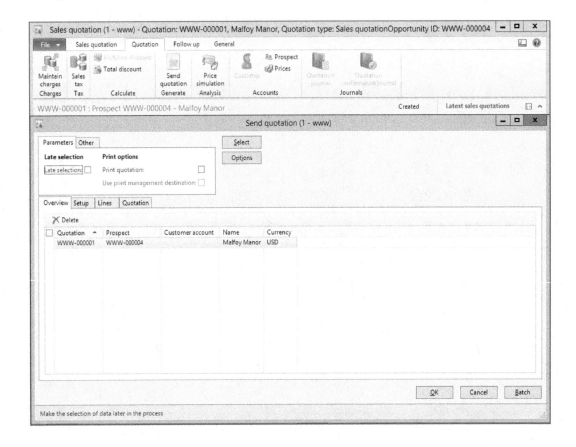

Note: If you configure **Print Management** then this will allow you to automatically e-mail this document when you generate it.

Creating Quotations For Opportunities

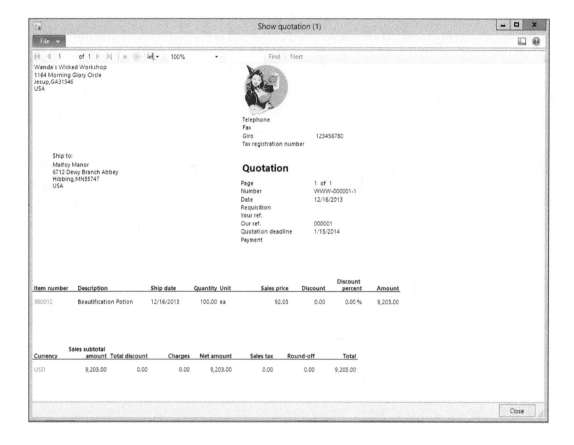

After you have sent the **Quotation,** the prospect should receive something that looks similar to this.

Converting A Quotation Into A Sales Order

When the **Prospect** accepts the quote, you will want to convert the **Quotation** into a **Sales Oder**. In order to do that, the **Prospect** also needs to be converted into a **Customer**. Also we need to close the Opportunity. Luckily that process is all automated within Dynamics AX and all you need to do is click a couple of buttons.

In this example we will show how to convert a **Quotation** into a **Sales Order**, and along the way tie up all of the loose ends.

Converting A Quotation Into A Sales Order

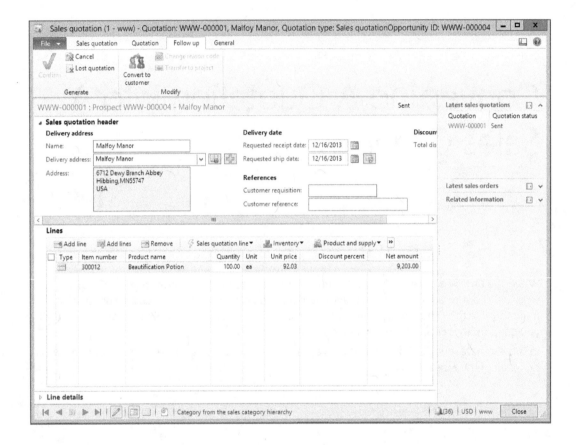

Open up the **Quotation** that you are firming up. Since this Quotation is associated with a prospect, you will notice that the **Confirm** menu button is grayed out.

Click on the **Convert to customer** button within the **Modify** group of the **Follow up** ribbon bar.

Converting A Quotation Into A Sales Order

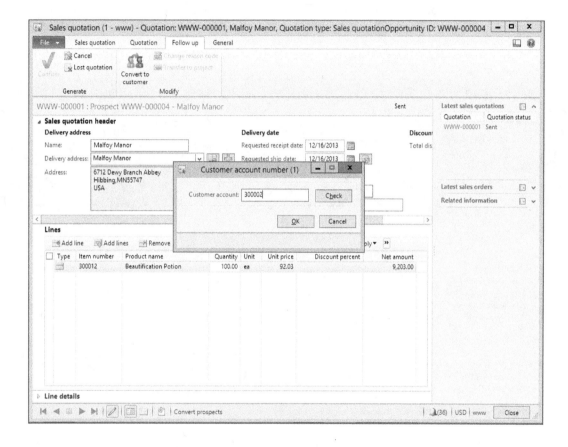

In this case, my customers are manually numbered so I need to assign a Customer account, and then click the **OK** button.

Converting A Quotation Into A Sales Order

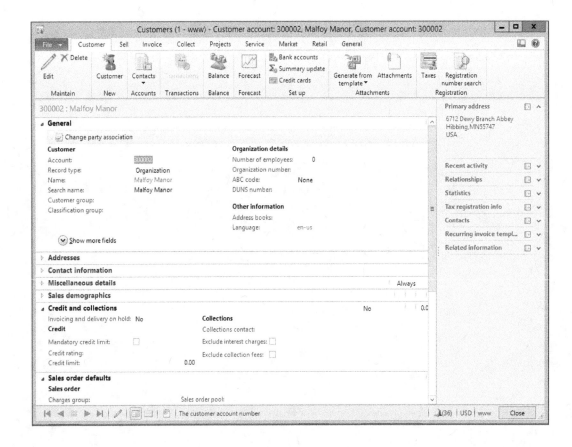

If we want, we can edit the **Customer** before continuing on.

Converting A Quotation Into A Sales Order

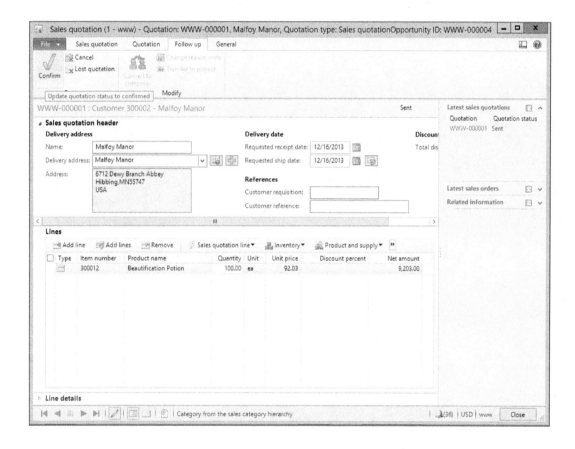

Now that the **Quotation** is associated with a **Customer**, click on the **Confirm** button within the **Generate** group on the **Follow Up** ribbon bar.

Converting A Quotation Into A Sales Order

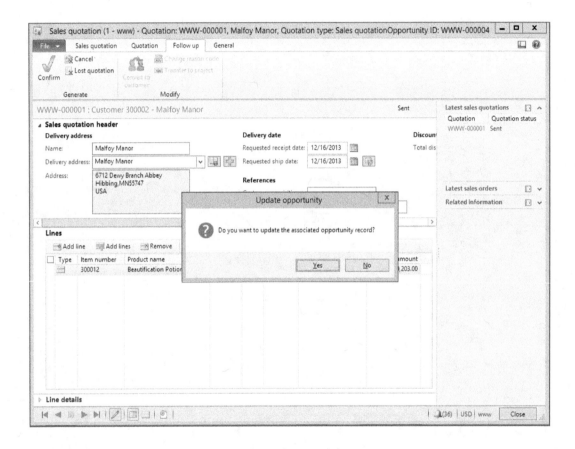

Dynamics AX will ask you if you want to update the **Opportunity**, mark it as **Won** and close it. Click **Yes**.

Converting A Quotation Into A Sales Order

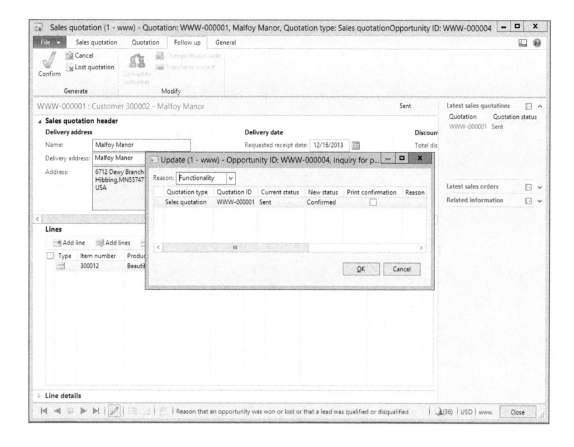

We can now specify the **Reason** for the win, and click the **OK** button.

Converting A Quotation Into A Sales Order

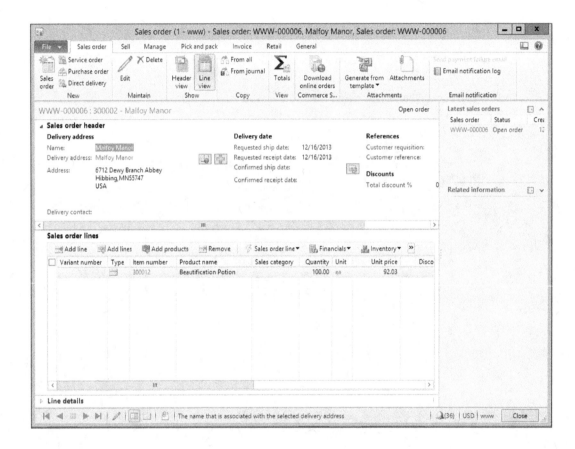

The new **Sales Order** will then be opened, with all of the information from the **Quotation** already populated.

Converting A Quotation Into A Sales Order

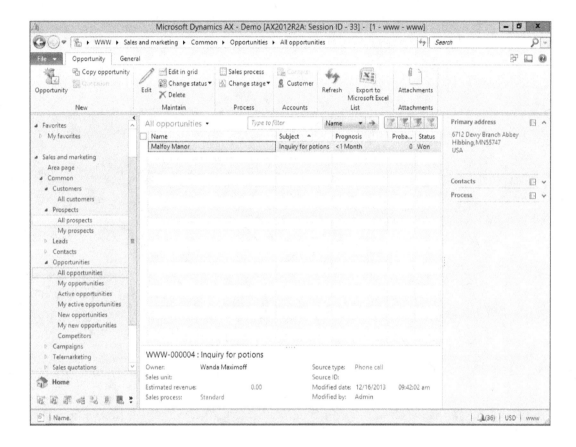

If we return to the **Opportunity** list page we will see that it has been marked as **Won** as well.

Creating Collaboration Workspaces For Opportunities

If you need to share information with your **Prospects** or **Customers** about the **Opportunities** then Dynamics AX has a solution for that. You can have the system create **Collaboration Workspaces** within SharePoint for you either automatically or on demand. These can have both internal and external access which means that you can share documents and plans with others through a central location that is linked back to the **Opportunity** records within Dynamics AX.

In this section we will show you how you can create **Collaboration Workspaces** directly from **Opportunities.**

Creating Collaboration Workspaces For Opportunities

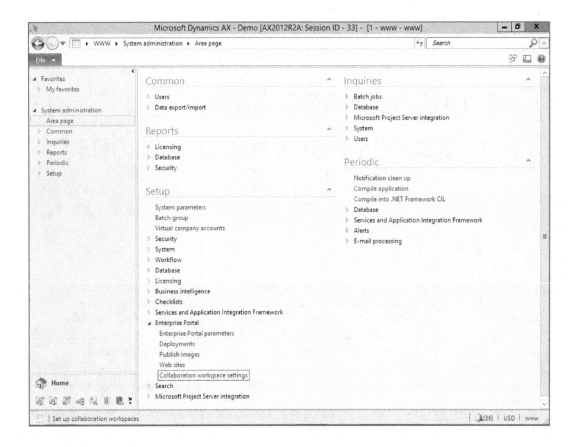

Before you start, you just need to make sure that Dynamics AX is configured to create the **Collaboration Workspaces**. To do this, click on the **Collaboration workspace settings** menu item within the **Enterprise Portal** folder of the **Setup** group within the **System administration** area page.

Creating Collaboration Workspaces For Opportunities

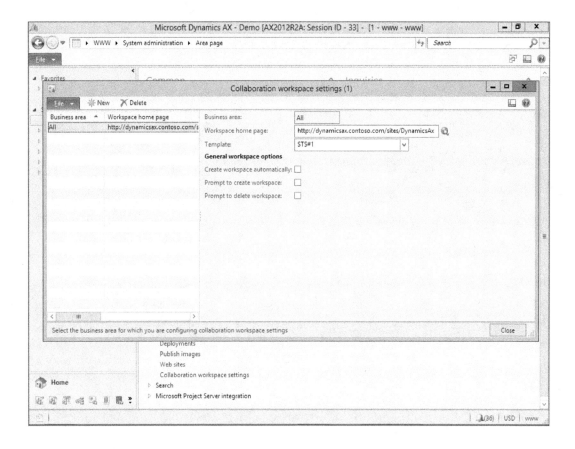

Make sure that you have a Business Area linked to your SharePoint collaboration workspace.

Creating Collaboration Workspaces For Opportunities

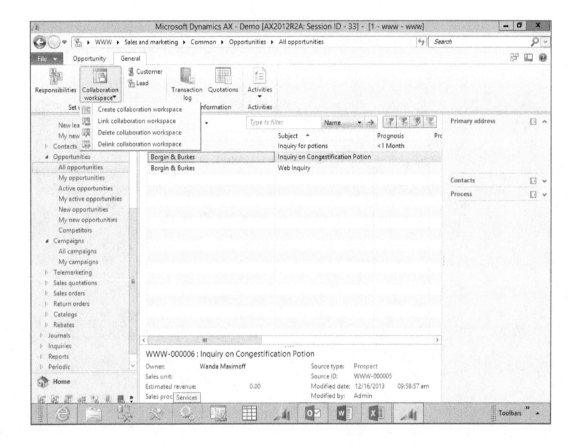

From either the **Opportunities** list or detail page click on the **Create collaboration workspace** menu item under the **Collaboration workspace** menu button within the **Set up** group of the **General** ribbon bar.

Creating Collaboration Workspaces For Opportunities

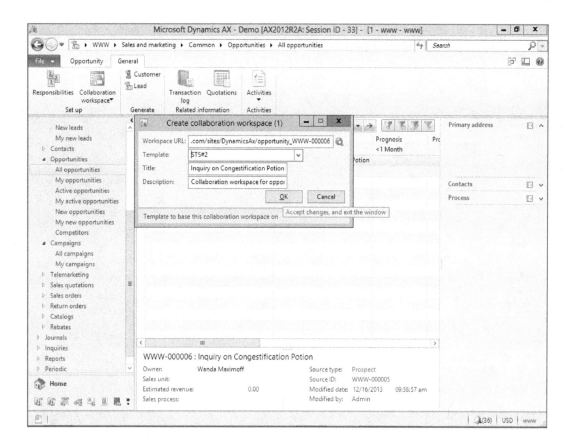

When the **Create collaboration workspace** dialog box is displayed, you can select any **Template** from SharePoint that you want to use for the collaboration workspace, and then click the **OK** button.

Creating Collaboration Workspaces For Opportunities

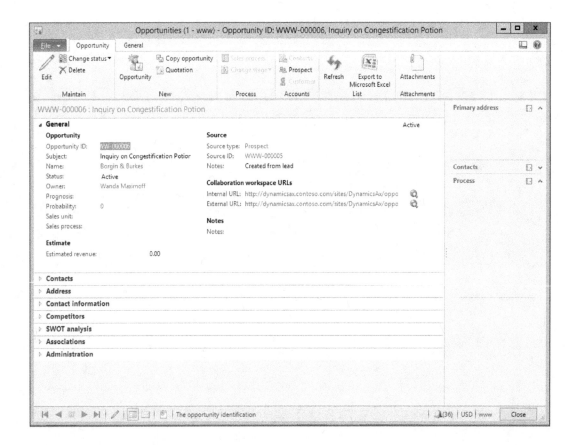

When you return to the **Opportunity,** you will notice that the **Collaboration workspace URL's** are now populated.

Creating Collaboration Workspaces For Opportunities

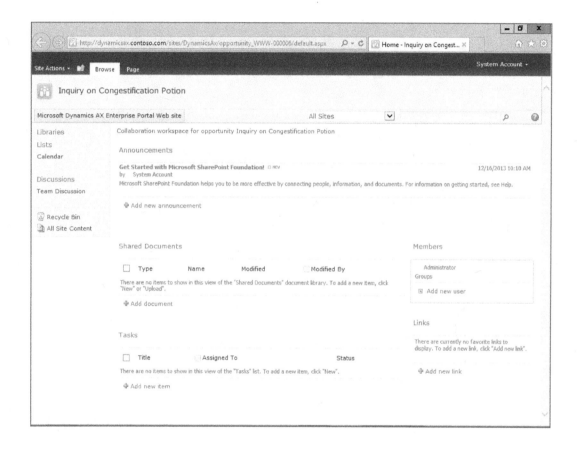

If you click on either of them, you will be taken to the **Collaboration Workspace** that was created for the **Opportunity.**

CONFIGURING LEAD MANAGEMENT

If you are marketing through lists, or if you are feeding Sales and Marketing through a Lead Acquisition tool, then you will probably want to take advantage of the **Lead Management** functionality in Dynamics AX. This allows you to create or import **Leads** and then pre-qualify them before they become **Opportunities.** They also have an added benefit that they create corresponding **Prospect** records automatically which you can update as the **Lead** is being qualified.

In this chapter we will show how you can configure and use the **Lead Management** functions within Dynamics AX.

Defining Lead Types

First we will want to set up some **Lead Types** so that we can segregate out the leads by source. This will allow us also to focus on certain channels when we are qualifying the leads.

In this example we will show how you can define your **Lead Types.**

Defining Lead Types

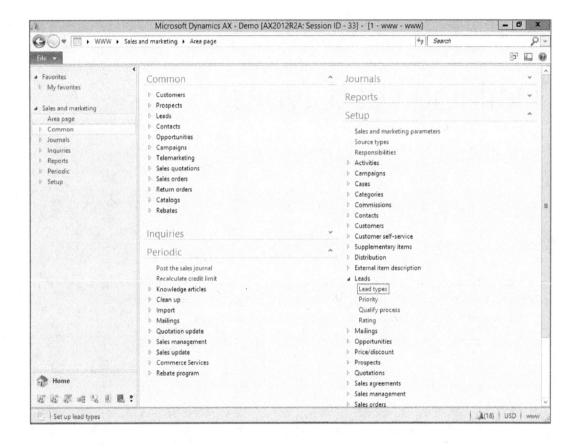

Select the **Lead Types** menu item from within the **Leads** folder of the **Setup** group of the **Sales and Marketing** area page.

Defining Lead Types

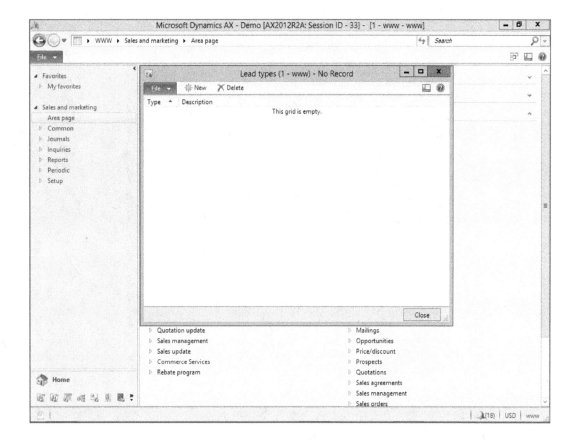

When the **Lead Types** maintenance form is displayed, click on the **New** button in the menu bar to add a new record.

Defining Lead Types

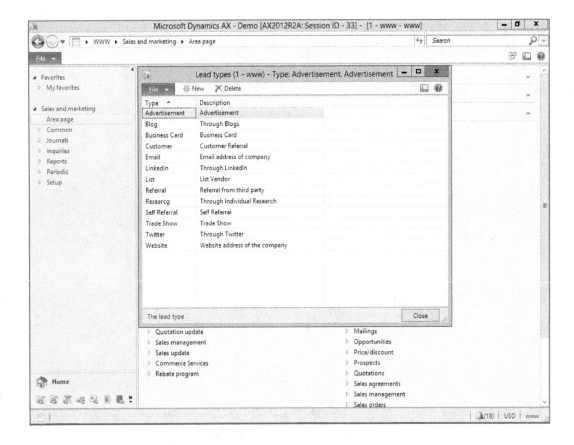

When you have finished setting up your **Lead Types** click on the **Close** button to exit the form.

Defining Lead Priorities

Although all **Leads** are important, some are more important than others. To identify this we will define a set of **Lead Priorities** that will allow us to prioritize leads as they are acquired so that we can focus on the best ones.

In this example we will show how you can define a set of **Lead Priority** codes.

Defining Lead Priorities

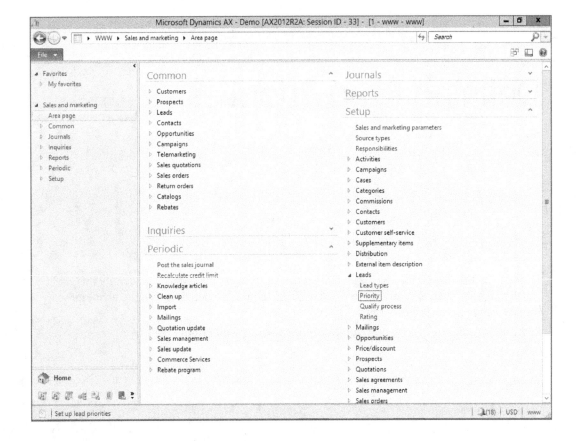

Select the **Priority** menu item from within the **Leads** folder of the **Setup** group of the **Sales and Marketing** area page.

Defining Lead Priorities

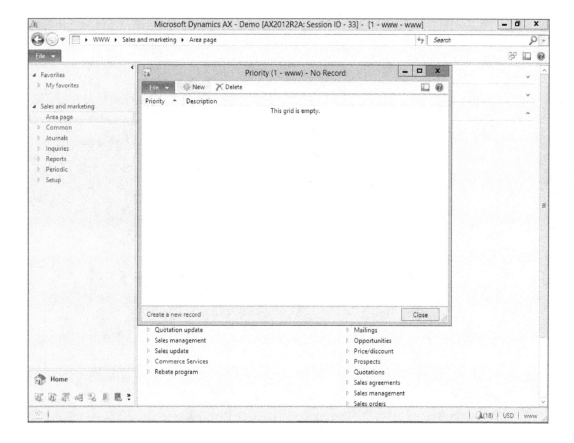

When the **Priority** maintenance form is displayed, click on the **New** button in the menu bar to add a new record.

Defining Lead Priorities

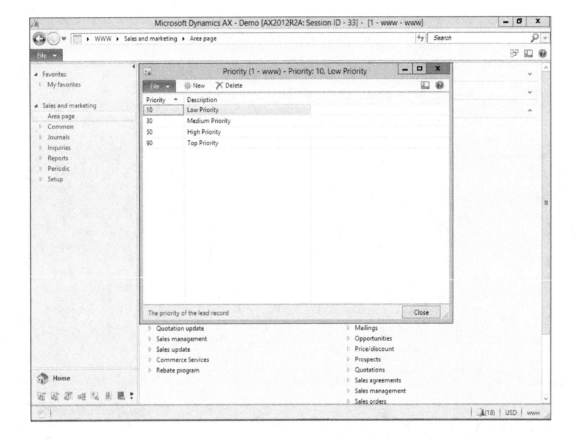

When you have finished setting up your **Priorities** click on the **Close** button to exit the form.

Defining Lead Ratings

As we work through the **Leads** we will probably be able to identify that some leads are of a higher quality than others. To allow us to record this we will also define a set of **Lead Ratings** that we can use throughout the process to assign a more subjective review of the value of the leads.

In this example we will show how to define a set of **Lead Rating** codes.

Defining Lead Ratings

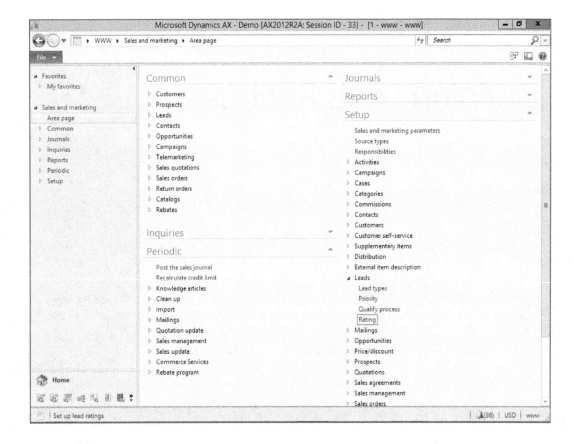

Select the **Rating** menu item from within the **Leads** folder of the **Setup** group of the **Sales and Marketing** area page.

Defining Lead Ratings

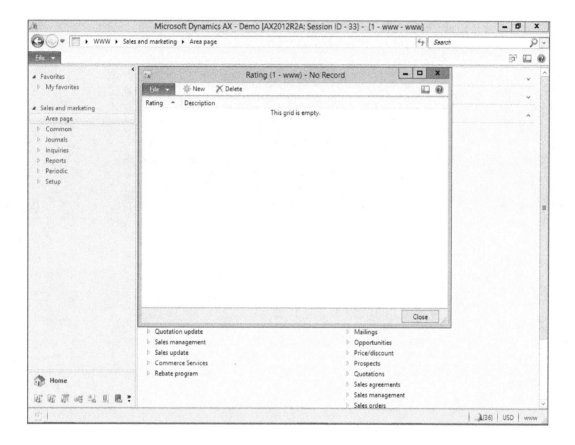

When the **Rating** maintenance form is displayed, click on the **New** button in the menu bar to add a new record.

Defining Lead Ratings

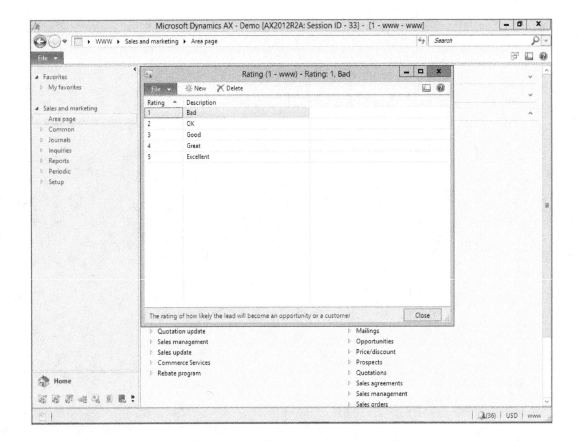

When you have finished setting up your **Ratings** click on the **Close** button to exit the form.

Configuring Lead Qualification Processes

Just like **Opportunities**, **Leads** can have a formal qualification process assigned to them that allows you to follow a standard sales policy when working **Leads**

In this example we will show how to configure a **Lead Qualification Process**.

Configuring Lead Qualification Processes

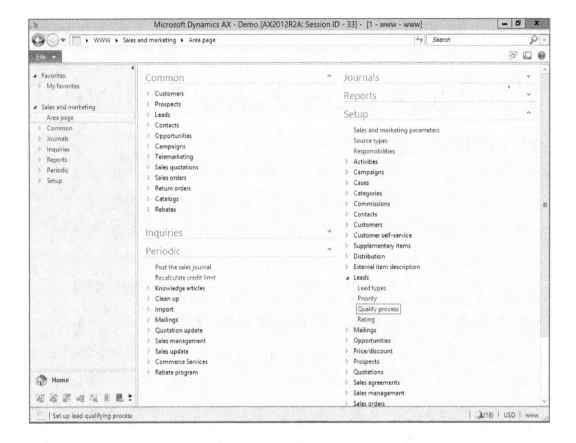

Select the **Qualify Process** menu item from within the **Leads** folder of the **Setup** group of the **Sales and Marketing** area page.

Configuring Lead Qualification Processes

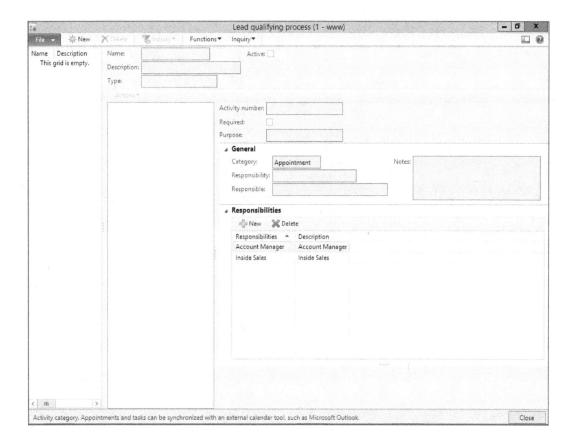

When the **Lead Qualification** designer is displayed, click on the **New** button in the menu bar to create a new **Lead Qualification Process**.

Configuring Lead Qualification Processes

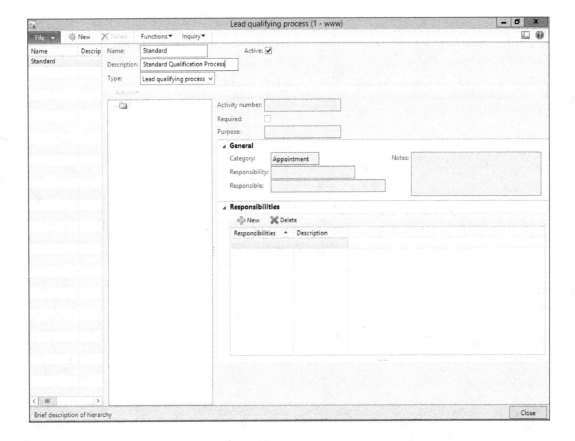

Give your **Qualification Process** a **Name**, and **Description** and then save the record.

Configuring Lead Qualification Processes

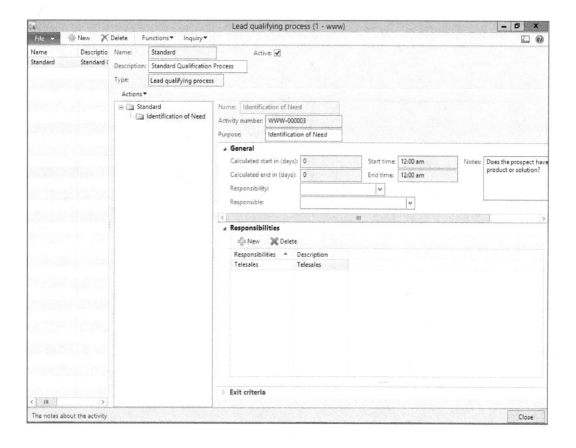

This will create a base node for your **Qualification Process** along with the first stage, which you can give a **Purpose** and specify **Notes.**

Configuring Lead Qualification Processes

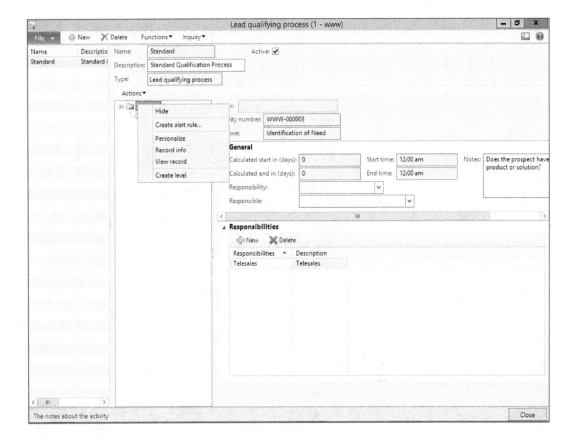

To create additional stages, just right-mouse-click on the root node, and select the **Create level** menu option.

Configuring Lead Qualification Processes

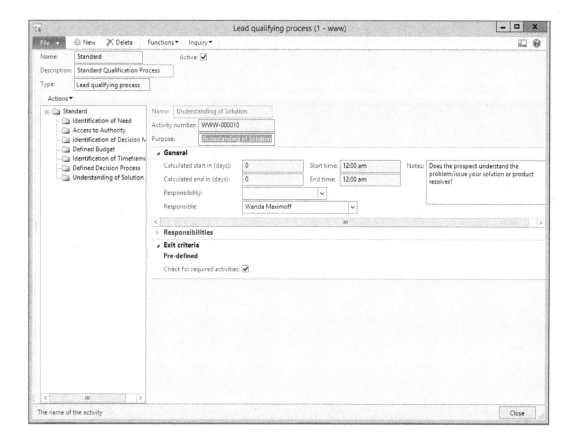

You can repeat this process for each of the steps in the qualification process. When you are done, you can click on the **Close** button to exit the form.

Creating New Leads

Once you have configured all of the base codes and processes for **Lead Management**, you can start creating new **Lead** records.

In this example we will show how to create a new **Lead**.

Creating New Leads

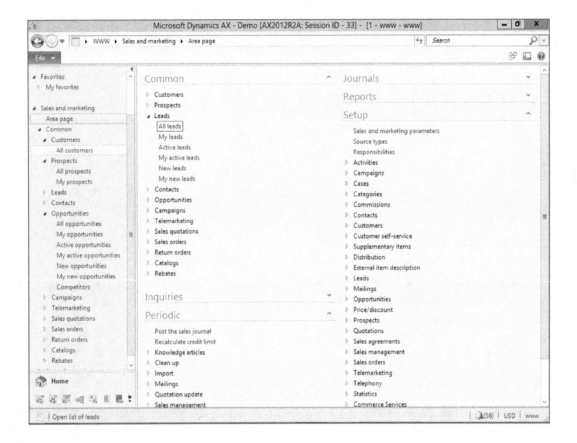

Select the **All Leads** menu item from within the **Leads** folder of the **Common** group of the **Sales and Marketing** area page.

Creating New Leads

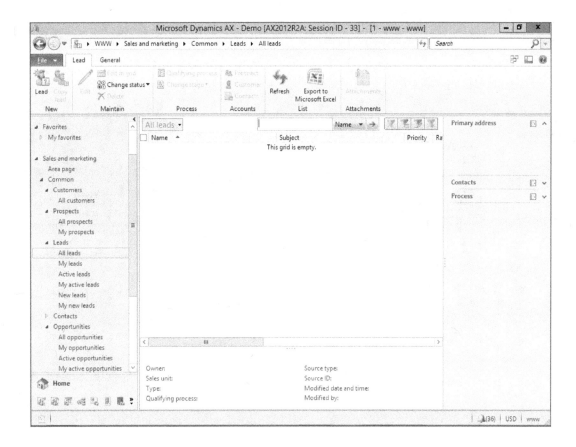

Click on the **Lead** button within the **New** group of the **Leads** ribbon bar.

Creating New Leads

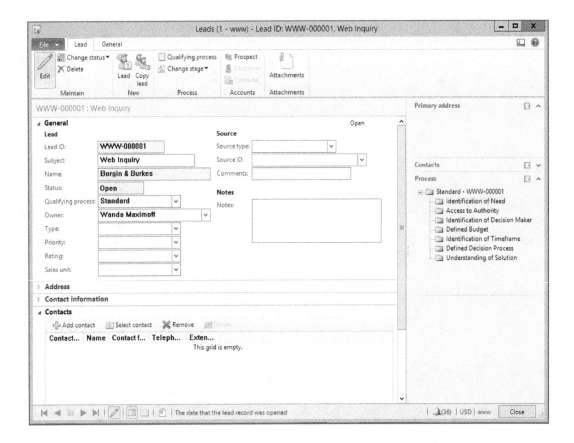

When the **Leads** form is displayed, enter a description of the **Lead** into the **Subject** field, and also enter in the **Name** associated with the lead.

Note: Although you are able to look up existing records for the **Name** field, you do not have to use one. If you enter in a **Name** that does not match any of the existing records, the lead will automatically create a new **Prospect** record for you.

Also you can associate a default **Qualifying Process** for the lead which will allow you to see the Process steps within the Factbox pane.

If you want to rate the **Lead** at this point as well, you can assign a **Type, Priority**, and a **Rating** to the **Lead.**

When you are finished, just click on the **Close** button to exit out of the form.

Creating New Leads

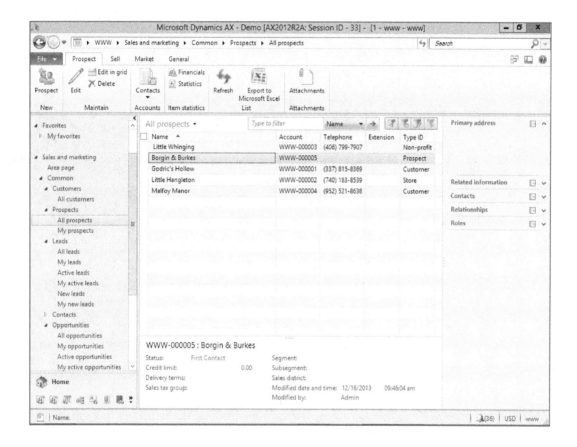

If you look at the **Prospects** list page, you will notice that a new record has been automatically added there to match the name that you assigned to the **Lead.**

Creating An Opportunity From A Lead

After a **Lead** has been qualified, then the next step in the process it to create an **Opportunity** that you can start showing on your Sale Pipeline. With Dynamics AX this is an extremely simple process.

In this example we will show how to create an **Opportunity** from a **Lead.**

Creating An Opportunity From A Lead

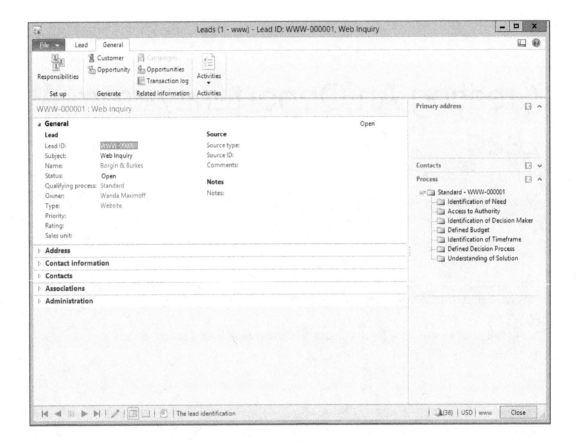

Open up the **Lead** record that you want to convert to an **Opportunity,** and click on the **Opportunity** button within the **Generate** group of the **General** ribbon bar.

Creating An Opportunity From A Lead

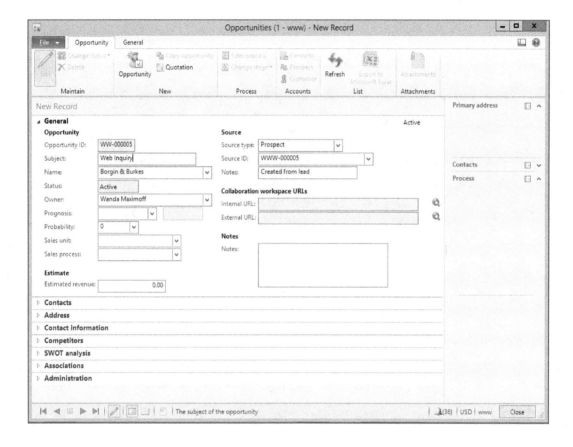

This will create an **Opportunity** record for you and copy over all of the information from the **Lead** without you having to do anything else.

CONFIGURING CAMPAIGN MANAGEMENT

Once you have a base of contacts within Dynamics AX you will probably want to create **Campaigns** around them for Sales and Marketing promotions. Dynamics AX manages this within the **Campaigns** area, allowing you to create new **Campaigns** managed through predefined **Sales Processes,** create target accounts to be associated with the campaigns, and then send e-mails out to the contacts publicizing the **Campaigns.**

In this chapter we will show how to configure and use the **Campaigns** functionality within Dynamics AX.

Defining Campaign Groups

First we will define some **Campaign Groups** to segregate out our campaigns by use and/or purpose. This allows us to report of the different **Campaign Groups** to track their effectiveness. In this example we will show how to define **Campaign Groups**.

Defining Campaign Groups

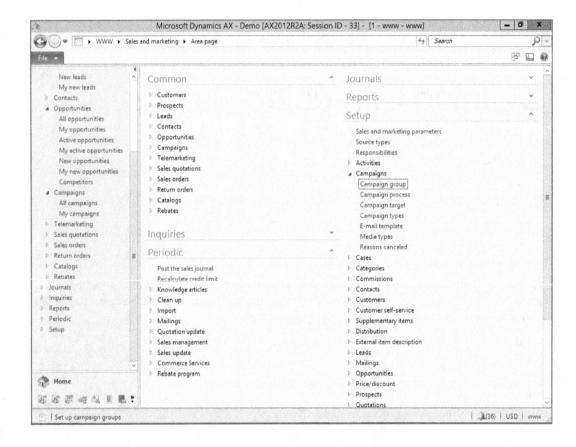

Select the **Campaign Groups** menu item from within the **Campaigns** folder of the **Setup** group of the **Sales and Marketing** area page.

Defining Campaign Groups

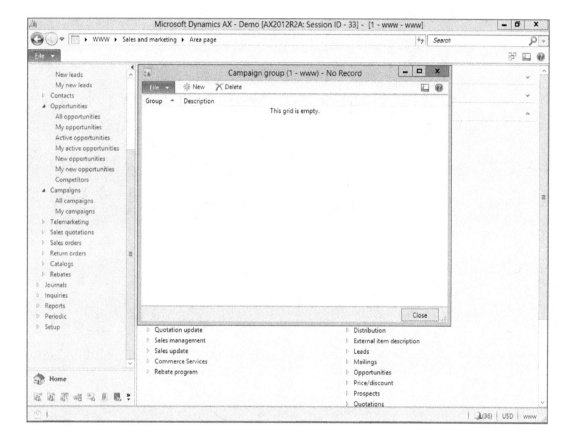

When the **Campaign group** maintenance form is displayed, click on the **New** button in the menu bar to add a new record.

Defining Campaign Groups

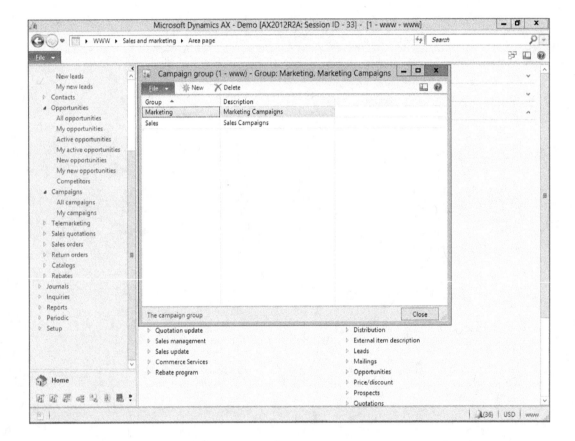

When you have finished setting up your **Campaign Groups** click on the **Close** button to exit the form.

Defining Campaign Types

We will also want to create some **Campaign Types** within Dynamics AX. These will identify the channel that we are using for our **Campaigns** such as Advertising, Social Media etc. When we report off our campaigns later on we will be able to use this information to track the effectiveness of the channels over multiple **Campaigns** and **Campaign Groups.**

In this example we will show how to define some typical **Campaign Types.**

Defining Campaign Types

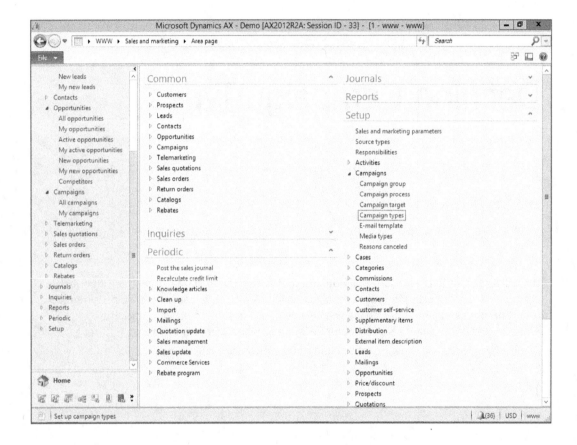

Select the **Campaign Types** menu item from within the **Campaigns** folder of the **Setup** group of the **Sales and Marketing** area page.

Defining Campaign Types

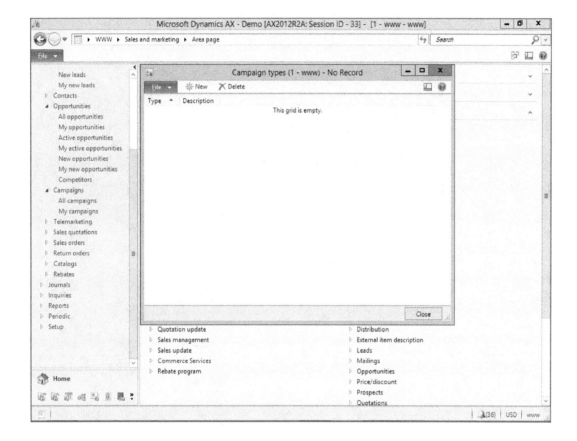

When the **Campaign Types** maintenance form is displayed, click on the **New** button in the menu bar to add a new record.

Defining Campaign Types

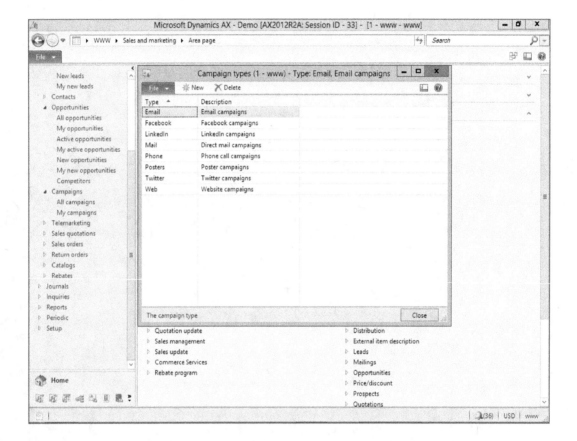

When you have finished setting up your **Campaign Types** click on the **Close** button to exit the form.

Defining E-mail Categories

We will also want to define our **E-mail Categories**. These will be used within the e-mailing functions of the **Campaigns** to classify the different types of mailings that we will be preforming.

In this example we will show how to define some sample **E-mail Categories.**

Defining E-mail Categories

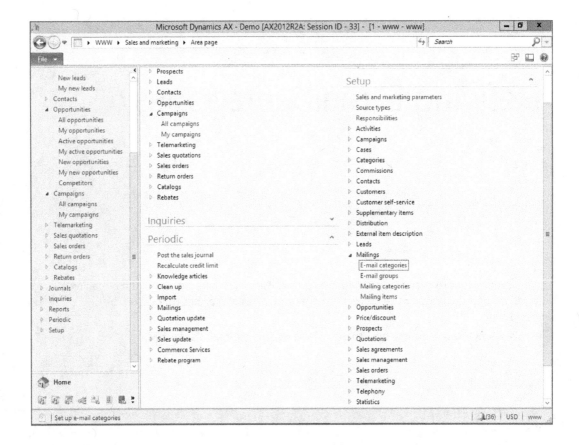

Click on the **E-mail Categories** menu item within the **Mailings** folder of the **Setup** group of the **Sales and Marketing** area page.

Defining E-mail Categories

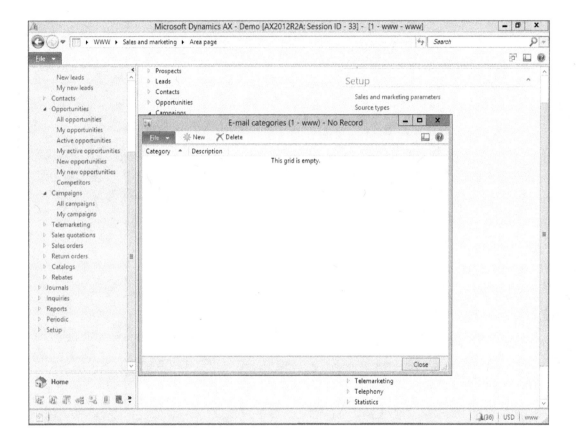

When the **E-mail Categories** maintenance form is displayed, click on the **New** button in the menu bar to add a new record.

Defining E-mail Categories

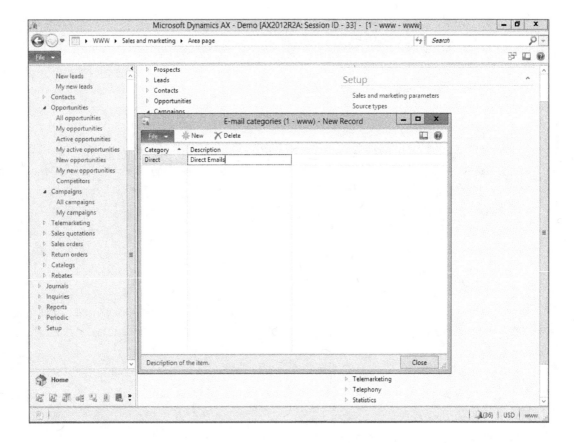

When you have finished setting up your **E-mail Categories** click on the **Close** button to exit the form.

Configuring Campaign Processes

Just like the **Leads** and **Opportunities** you can define processes for the **Campaigns** that allow you to specify the typical steps that you would use as you are designing and executing **Campaigns**. This also allow you to associate tasks and appointments in much the same way as the other process designers, allowing you to automate much of the **Campaign** management.

In this example we will show you how you can design a **Campaign Process** to manage your **Campaigns.**

Configuring Campaign Processes

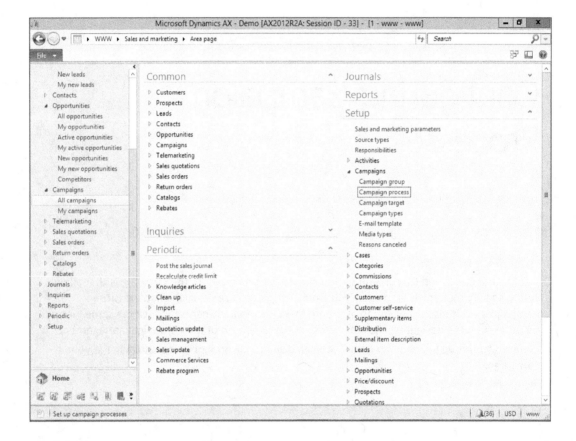

Click on the **Campaign process** menu item within the **Campaigns** folder of the **Setup** groups of the **Sales and Marketing** area page.

Configuring Campaign Processes

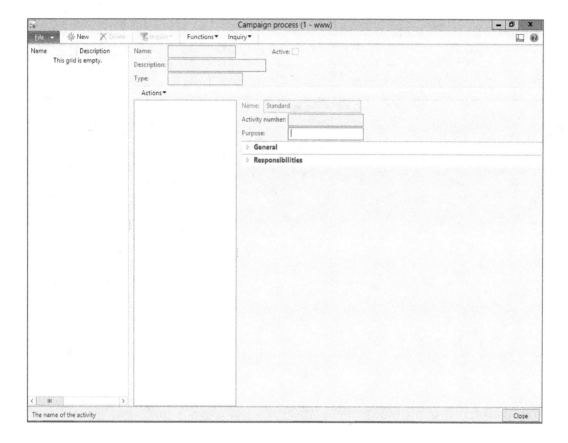

When the **Campaign Process** designer is displayed, click on the **New** button in the menu bar to create a new **Campaign process.**

Configuring Campaign Processes

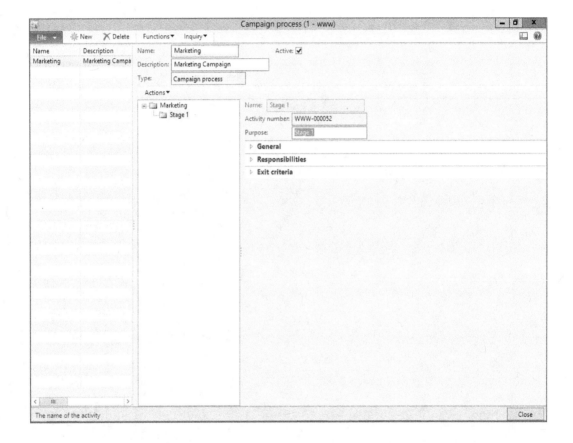

Give your **Campaign Process** a **Name** and **Description**, and then save it. This will create the root node for your **Campaign Process** and also the first stage in the process.

Configuring Campaign Processes

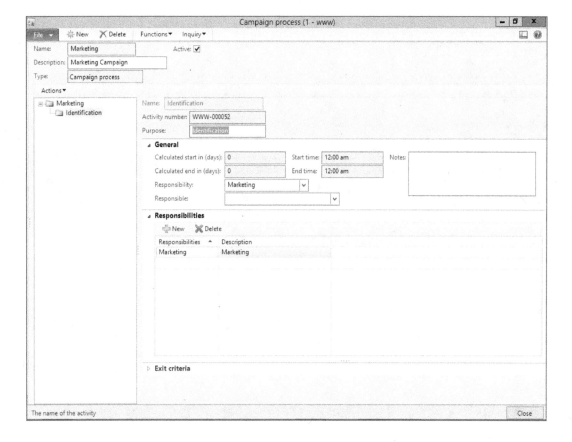

Give your first stage a **Purpose** and if you want to give a description of the stage, you can enter that into the **Notes** field for the stage.

Configuring Campaign Processes

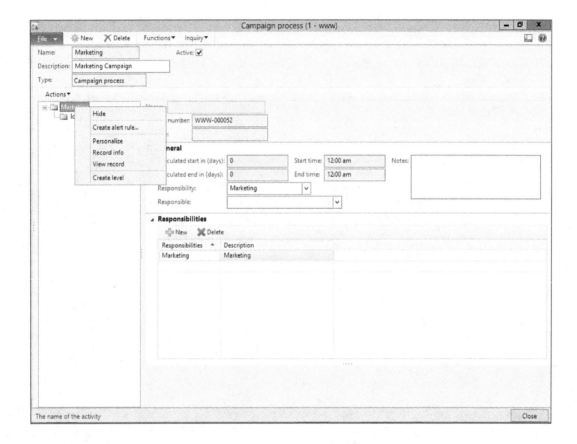

To add an additional step to the process, just right-mouse-click on the root node within the process tree, and select the **Create level** option.

Configuring Campaign Processes

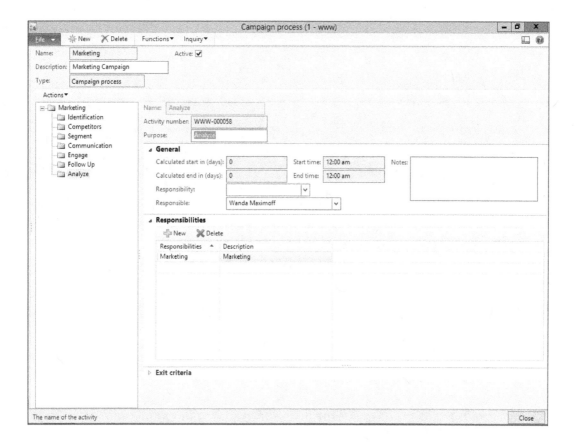

Repeat the process until you have all of the stages defined in your **Campaign Process** and then click the **Close** button to exit the form.

Copying Stages And Activities From Other Campaign Processes

If you want to use a new **Campaign Process** which is similar to an existing one, except for a couple of tweaks, rather than modifying the original **Campaign Process**, you can create a copy of the original one, and then make your changes to the copied version. This saves you from having to continually tweak existing **Campaign Processes** to meet your particular needs, and also saves you from redesigning **Campaign Processes** to create new ones.

In this example we will show you how you can copy existing **Campaign Processes** to create new variations.

Copying Stages And Activities From Other Campaign Processes

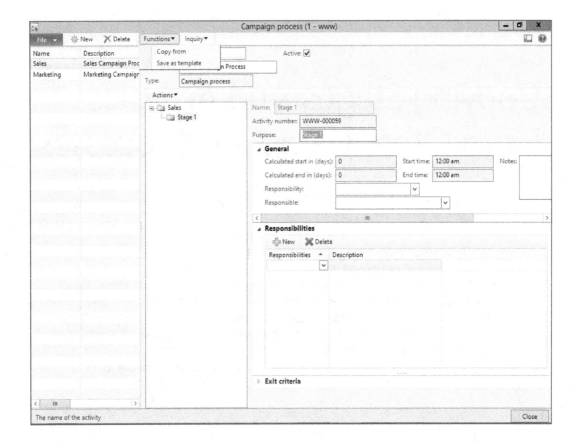

Select the **Campaign Process** that you want to copy to, and select the **Copy from** menu item from the **Functions** menu in the menu bar.

Copying Stages And Activities From Other Campaign Processes

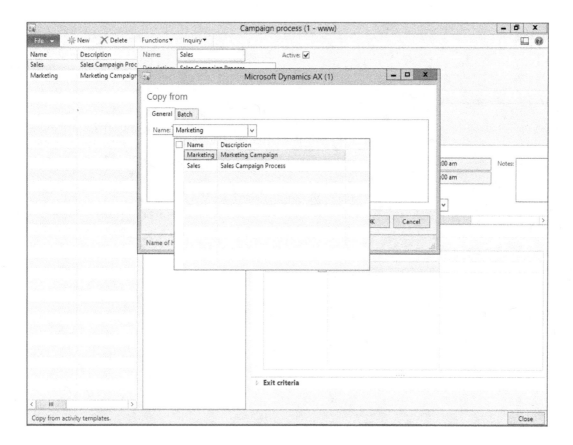

When the **Copy from** dialog box is displayed, select the **Campaign Process** that you want to use as the template and then click the **OK** button.

Copying Stages And Activities From Other Campaign Processes

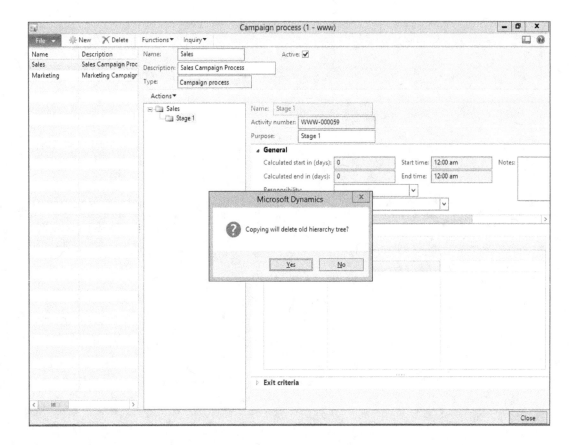

If you are sure that you want to overwrite the existing stages, then click the **OK** button on the confirmation dialog box.

Copying Stages And Activities From Other Campaign Processes

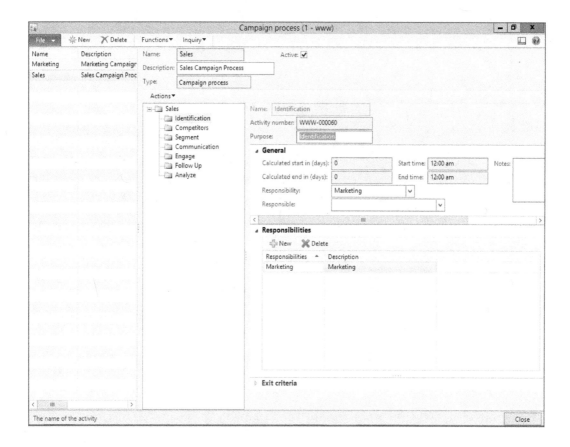

Now your new **Campaign Process** should have all the same steps as the original that you copied from.

Note: You can do this for all of the different Process Types within the Sales and Marketing area.

Configuring Campaign Parameters

To make sure that everything is as streamlined as possible with the **Campaigns** there are a few general parameters that we can configure within **Sales and Marketing** around the Campaign Management.

In this example we will show some configuration changes that you may want to make within the **Sales and Marketing** parameters.

Configuring Campaign Parameters

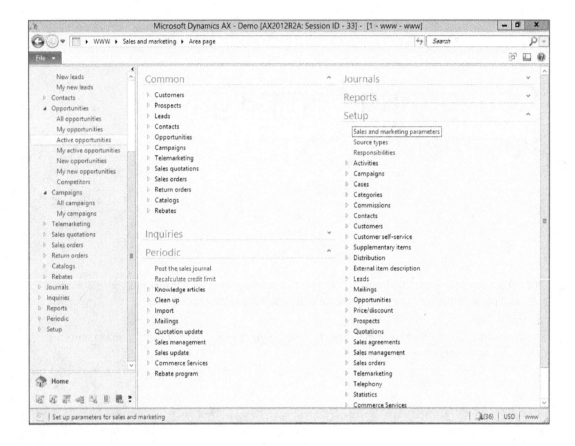

Click on the **Sales and Marketing Parameters** menu item within the **Setup** group of the **Sales and Marketing** area page.

Configuring Campaign Parameters

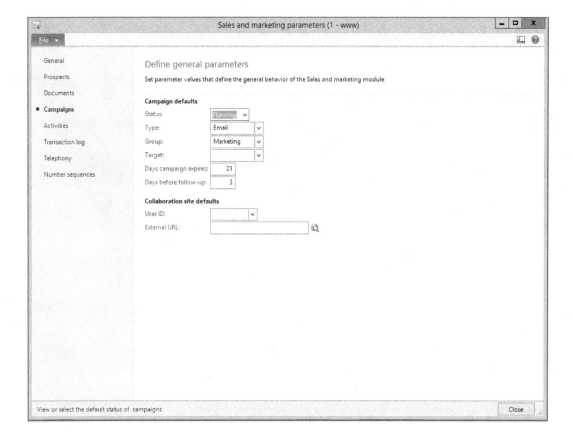

When the **Sales and Marketing** Parameters form is displayed, first select the **Campaigns** tab on the left.

You will want to set default values for the **Status**, **Type**, and also **Group** within the **Campaign defaults**.

Configuring Campaign Parameters

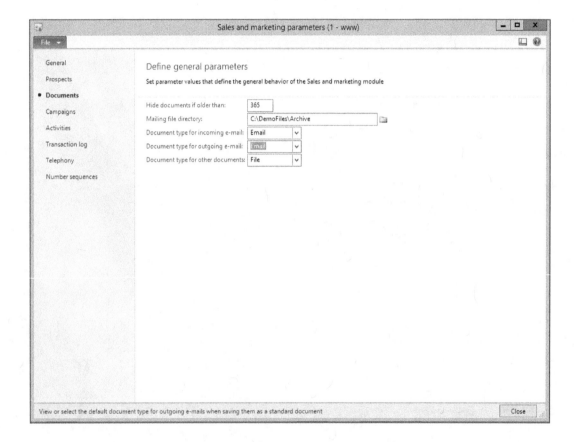

Also, select the **Documents** tab on the left, and make sure that you have the **Mailing file directory** defined so that you will be able to send e-mails, and also configure the three **Document Type** fields so that you have default document types for your Campaign communication.

When you have done that, click on the **Close** button to exit out of the form.

Configuring The System Archive Directory

One final check that we need to do before starting using our **Campaigns** is to make sure that you have the **System Archive Directory** defined. The Campaign Management process will use this as a temporary folder for all of your communication, so if this is not defined, then Dynamics AX will whine a little.

Configuring The System Archive Directory

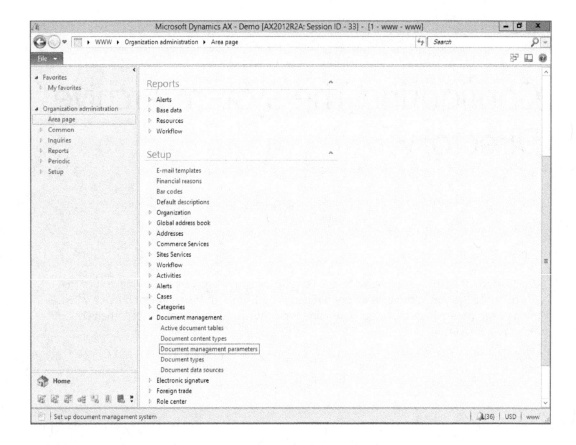

Click on the **Document management parameters** menu link within the **Document Management** folder of the **Setup** group of the **Organization Administration** area page.

Configuring The System Archive Directory

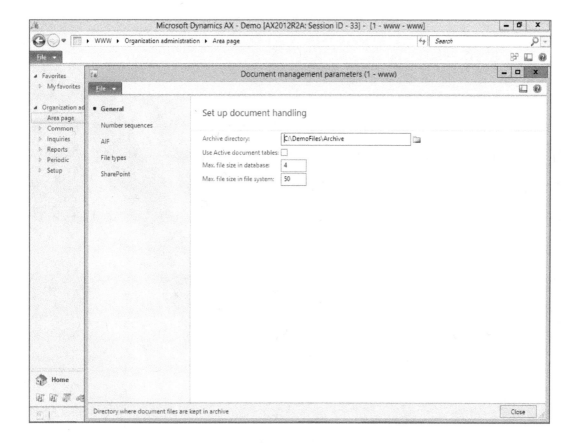

Make sure that you have a directory specified within the **Archive directory** field on the **General** tab.

Creating New Campaigns

Once all of the base codes and controls have been set up, you can start executing your **Campaigns** within Dynamics AX. The first step in this process is to create a new **Campaign.** In this example we will show you how to create a new **Campaign** record.

Creating New Campaigns

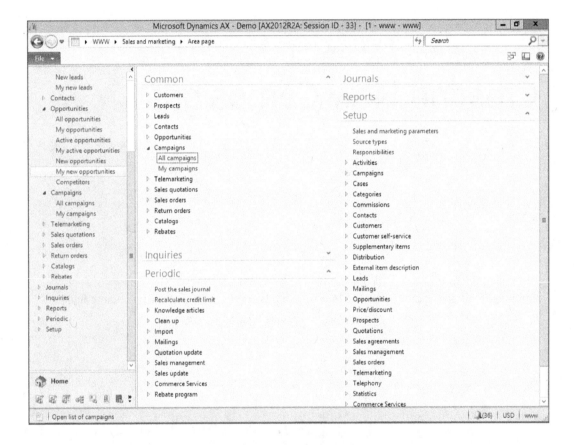

Click on the **All Campaigns** menu item within the **Campaigns** folder of the **Common** group within the **Sales and Marketing** area page.

Creating New Campaigns

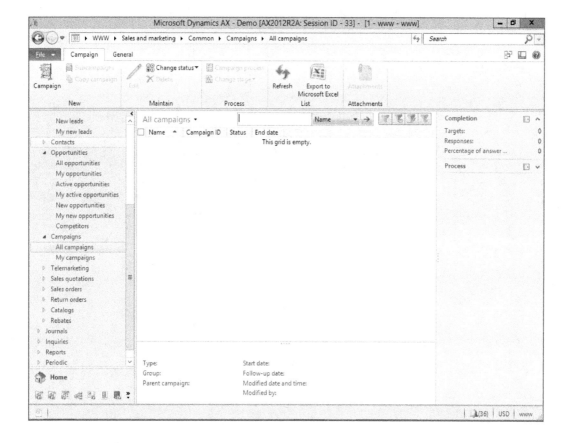

When the **Campaign** list page is displayed, click on the **Campaign** menu button within the **New** group of the **Campaign** ribbon bar.

Creating New Campaigns

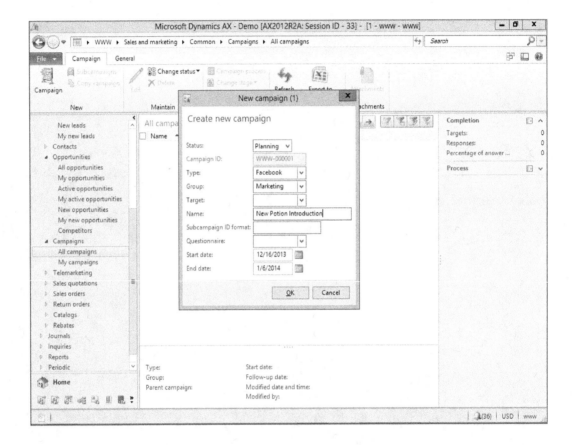

When the **New Campaign** quick entry form is displayed, fill in the **Status**, **Type**, **Group** and also **Name** for the campaign.

You can also specify the **Start date**, and **End date** as well before clicking the **OK** button to create the campaign.

Creating New Campaigns

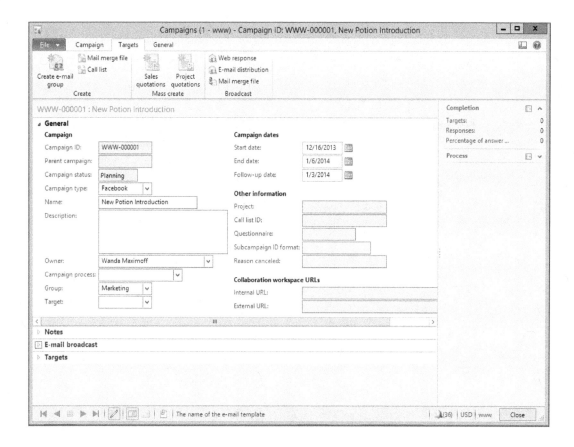

After you have done this you will be taken to the main data form for the **Campaign** where you can fill in more detailed information.

Selecting Target Contacts For Campaigns

Once you have created a campaign you can start allow Dynamics AX to select the **Contacts** that you want to contact about the campaign by using the **Target Selection** function that is part of the **Campaign Management**. This feature allows you to define one or more queries that describe the contacts that you want to select, and then it will search the database for all matches and then associate them with the **Campaign**.

In this example we will show you how to use the **Target Selection** function to assign **Contacts** to your **Campaigns.**

Selecting Target Contacts For Campaigns

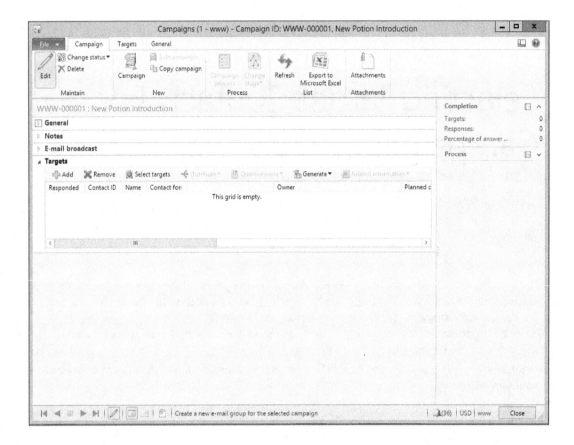

Open up your **Campaign,** and expand the **Targets** tab.

Then click on the **Select Targets** button within the tabs menu bar.

Selecting Target Contacts For Campaigns

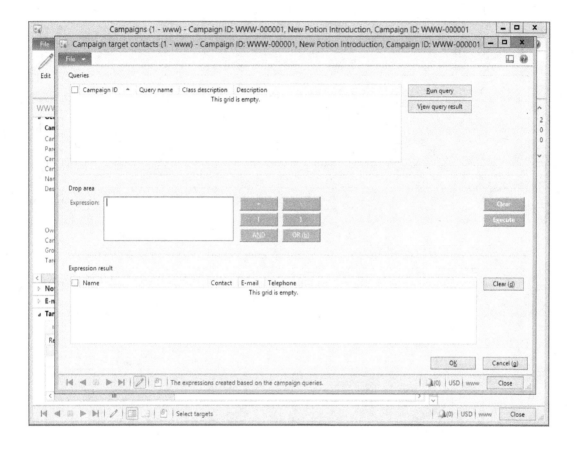

This will open up the Selection Query builder. To create a new query, either select **New** from the **File** menu, or press **CTRL+N**.

Selecting Target Contacts For Campaigns

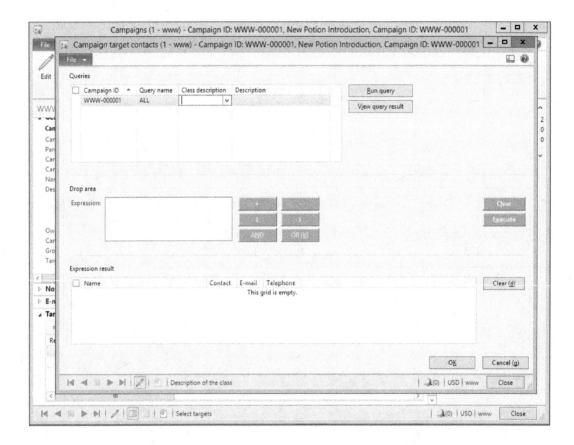

Assign your new **Query** a name (no spaces allowed) and then click on the dropdown on the **Class description** field.

Selecting Target Contacts For Campaigns

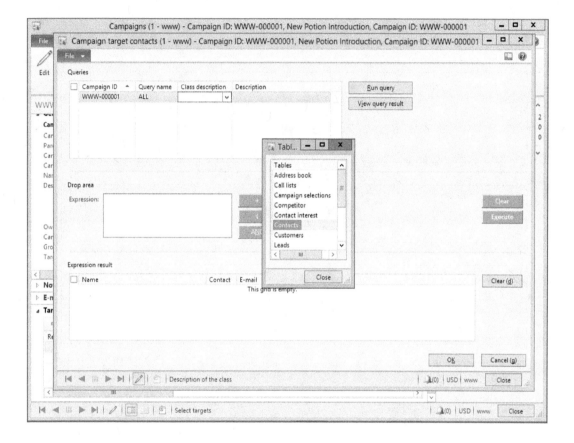

Select the **Table** that you want to search on with the **Query** and then click the **Close** button.

Selecting Target Contacts For Campaigns

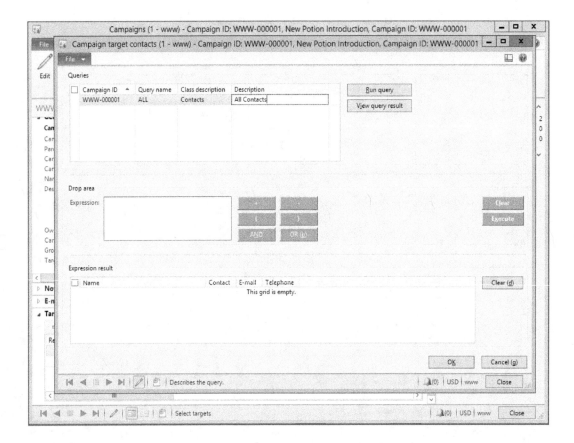

Finally, give your query a **Description**.

To refine your **Query**, click on the **Run query** button.

Selecting Target Contacts For Campaigns

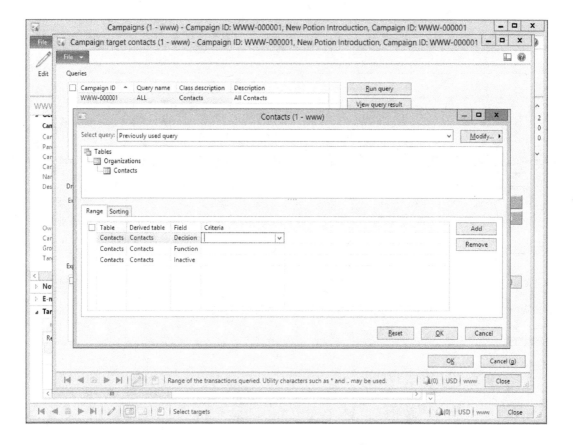

This will open up a selection designer box. You can add additional fields for the query, and also put wildcard selection criteria against any of the fields to filter out certain records.

When you have finished designing your query, click the **OK** button.

Selecting Target Contacts For Campaigns

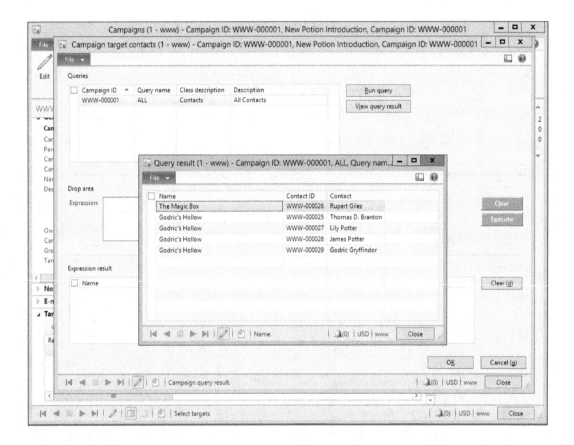

If you click on the **View Query Results** button within the **Target Selection** designer, then you will be able to see all of the results that match your query selection.

Selecting Target Contacts For Campaigns

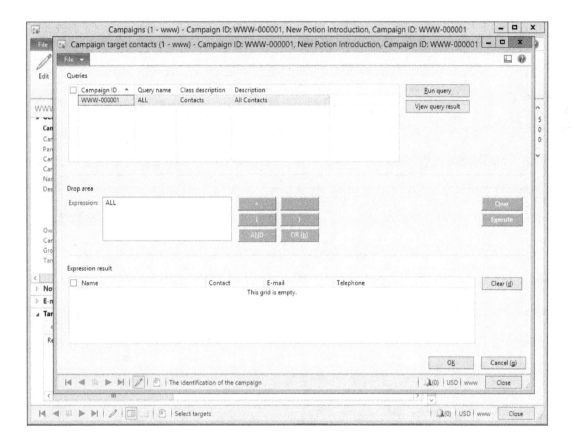

Now drag the query that you created into the **Drop Area Expression** list box to tell the system to use that query.

Note: You can create as many of these queries as you want for the **Campaign** and then join them together within the **Query Designer** to create more complicated selections and exclusions.

Selecting Target Contacts For Campaigns

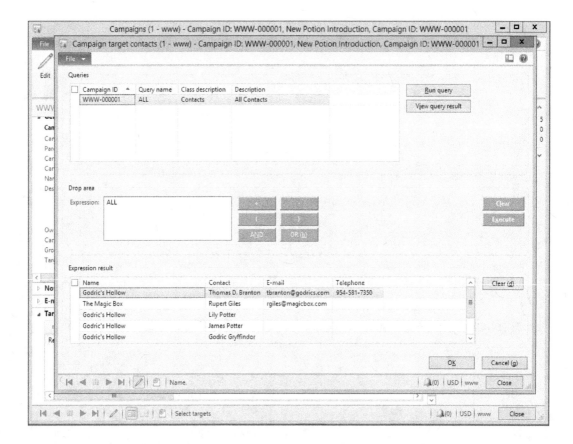

To check that your **Query** is working, click on the **Execute** button, and you will be able to see all of the matching contacts within the **Expression Results** table.

When you are happy with the results, just click on the **OK** button.

Selecting Target Contacts For Campaigns

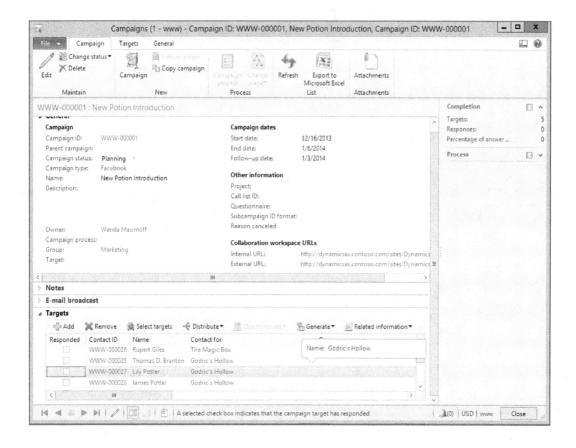

Now all of the targets that match the query will be added into the **Targets** list of the **Campaign.**

Creating E-mail Groups From Campaigns

Once you have created your **Target List** for your **Campaign**, you can then use the E-mailing functions within the **Sales and Marketing** module to send out mass e-mails around it. Before we do that though we will want to convert our target list into an **E-mail Group** that the mailing function will be able to use.

In this example we will show how you can create an **E-mail Group** from a **Campaign**.

Creating E-mail Groups From Campaigns

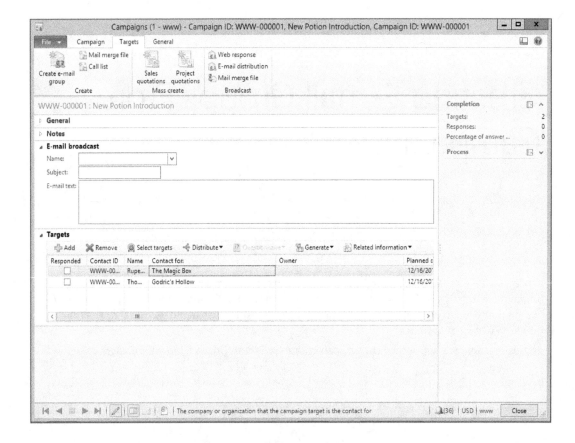

Open the **Campaign** that you want to create the e-mail group for and click on the **Create e-mail group** menu button within the **Create** group of the **Targets** ribbon bar.

Creating E-mail Groups From Campaigns

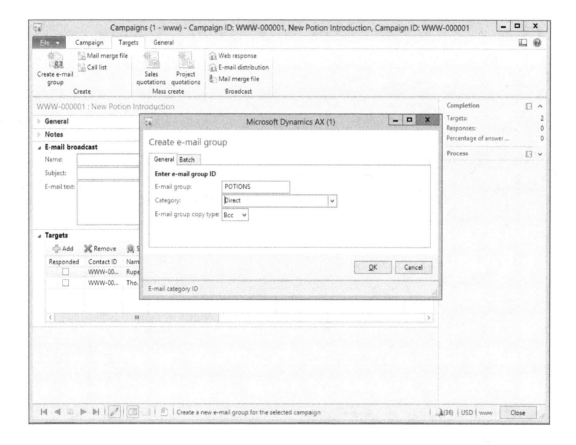

Assign a name in the **E-mail Group** field, and also assign an **E-mail Category** in the **Category** field.

When you have done that, click on the **OK** button to create the group.

Creating E-mail Groups From Campaigns

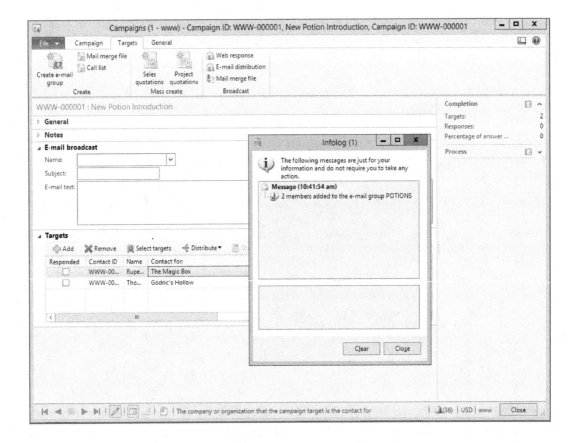

You should receive a notice that you have added new members to an **E-mail Group**.

Creating E-mail Groups From Campaigns

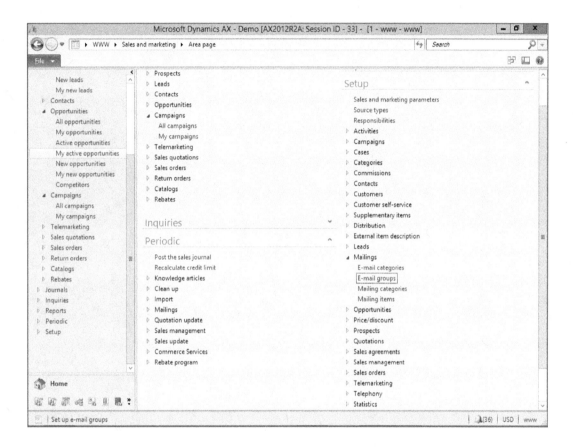

If you ever want to view the E-mail Groups that you create this way, you can click on the **E-mail Groups** menu item within the **Mailings** folder of the **Setup** group on the **Sales and Marketing** area page.

Creating E-mail Groups From Campaigns

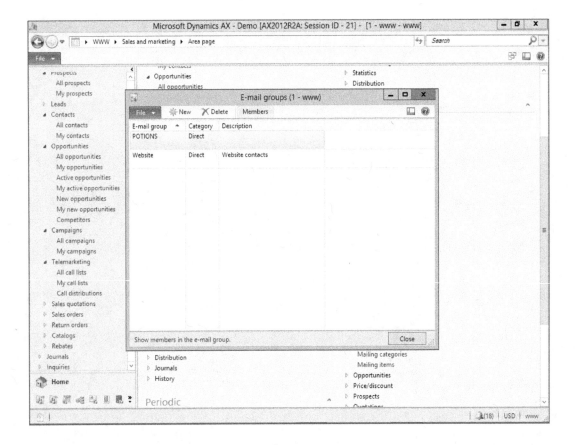

When the **E-mail Groups** maintenance form is displayed, you will be able to see the group that you just created.

Creating E-mail Groups From Campaigns

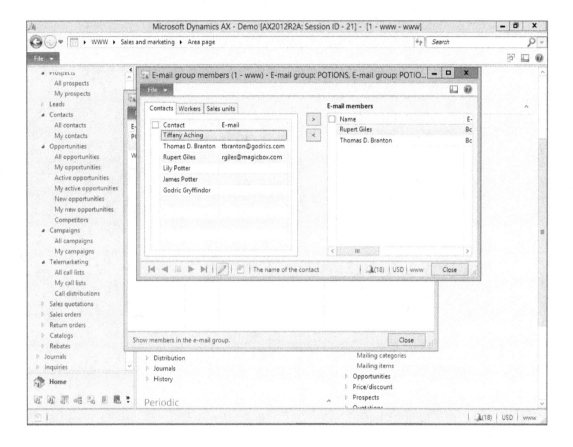

If you click on the **Members** button on the menu bar, then you will also be taken into the group designer where you will see the contacts that have been assigned to the **E-mail Group.**

Sending E-mail Distributions From A Campaign

Once you have created an **E-Mail Group** for your **Campaign**, you can start sending out emails associated with it.

In this example we will show how you can send emails directly from the Campaign to your targeted list.

Sending E-mail Distributions From A Campaign

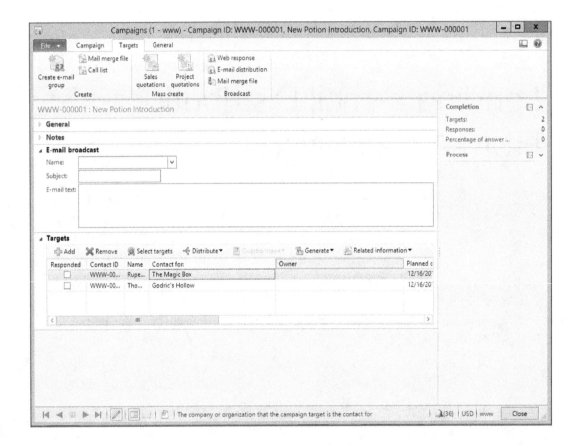

Open up the **Campaign** that you want to create the **E-Mailing** for and then click on the **E-mail distribution** menu button within the **Broadcasts** group of the **Targets** ribbon bar.

Sending E-mail Distributions From A Campaign

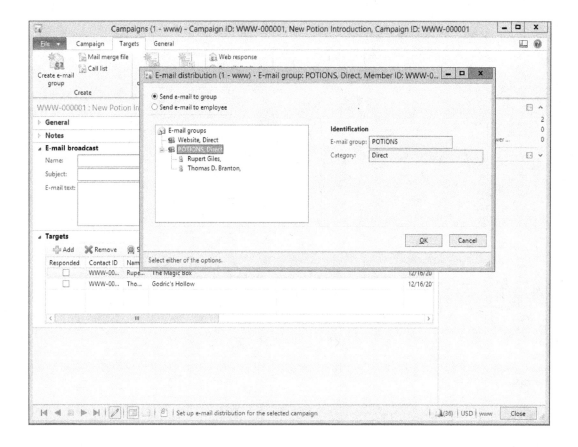

Select your **E-mail Group** that you want to send the e-mails to and then click on the **OK** button.

Sending E-mail Distributions From A Campaign

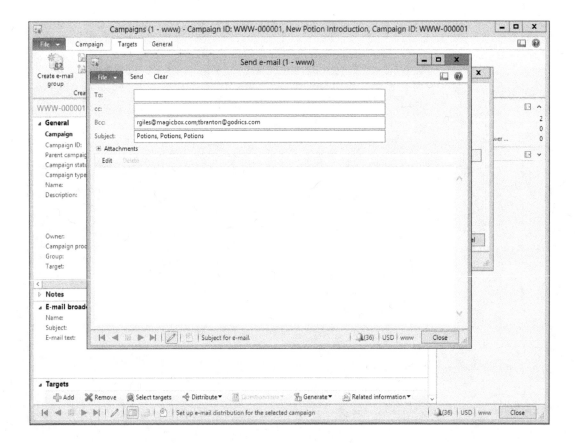

When the E-mail Template Designer is displayed, paste in any text that you may want to use in the broadcast, an then click on the **Send** button in the menu bar.

Sending E-mail Distributions From A Campaign

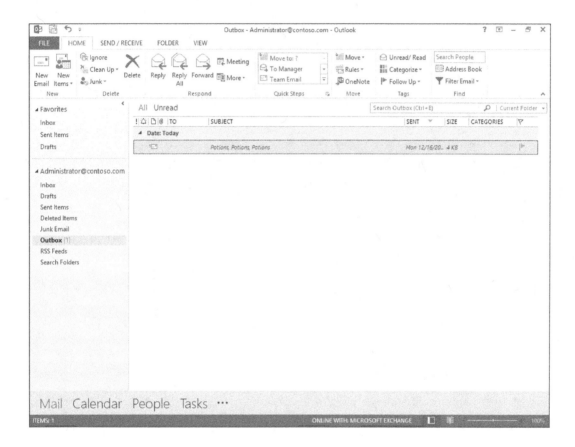

You will be able to track the e-mail being sent through your Outlook client.

CONFIGURING TELEMARKETING

The **Telemarketing** functions within the **Sales and Marketing** area of Dynamics AX allow you to manage then generation and distribution of call lists between users, and also gives you mechanisms like **Questionnaires** to help guide the information gathering process during the process.

In this chapter we will show how you can configure and use the **Telemarketing** functions within Dynamics AX.

Defining Telemarketing Cancellation Reason Codes

Before we start creating **Call Lists**, we need to configure some **Cancellation Reason Codes** so that we can track the reasons for aborted calls within the system.

In this section we will show how to define some example **Cancellation Reason Codes.**

Defining Telemarketing Cancellation Reason Codes

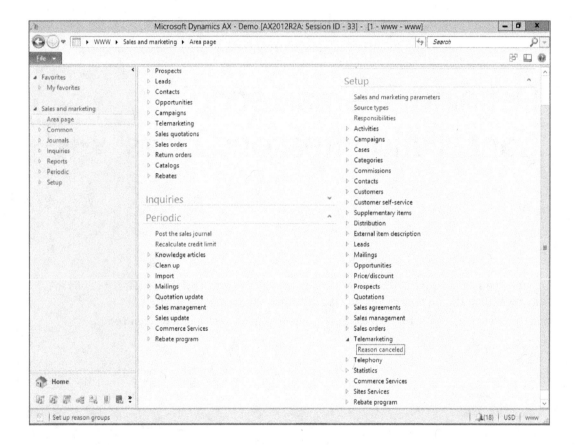

Click on the **Reason Cancelled** menu item within the **Telemarketing** folder of the **Setup** group within the **Sales and Marketing** area page.

Defining Telemarketing Cancellation Reason Codes

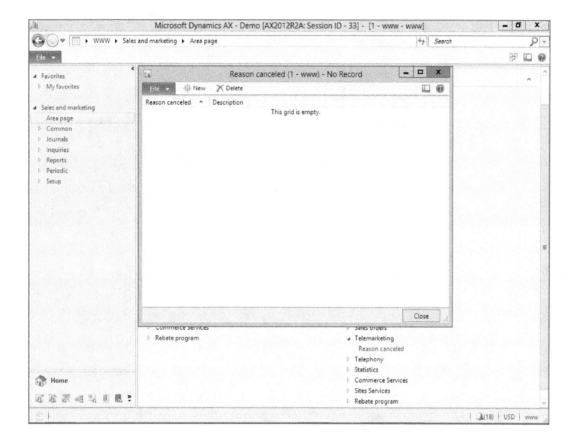

When the **Reason Cancelled** maintenance form is displayed, click on the **New** button in the menu bar to add a new record.

Defining Telemarketing Cancellation Reason Codes

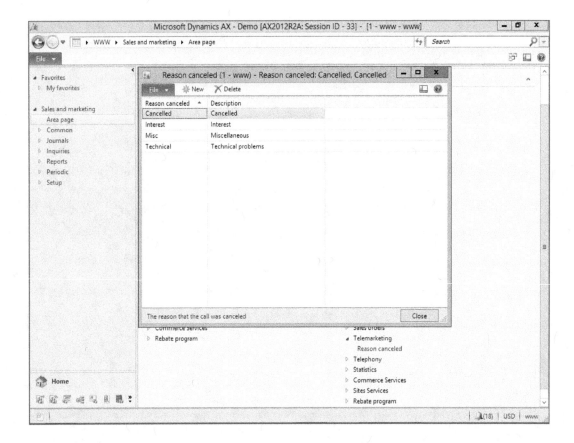

When you have finished setting up your **Reasons Cancelled** click on the **Close** button to exit the form.

Creating A New Call List

You can create **Call Lists** within **Sales and Marketing** from scratch pretty easily. You may want to do this for one-off call lists that are not assigned to any particular **Campaign** within the system.

In this example we will show how you can create new **Call Lists**.

Creating A New Call List

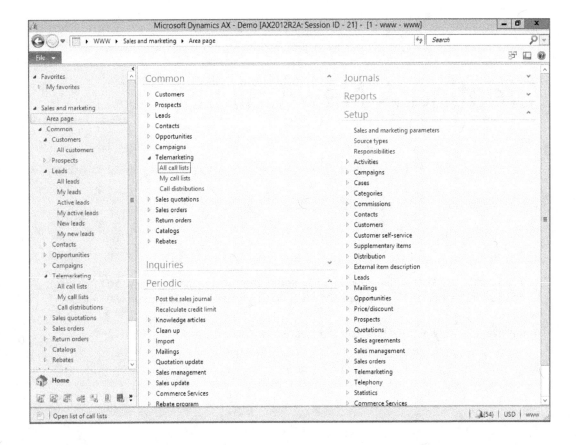

Click on the **All Call Lists** menu item within the **Telemarketing** folder of the **Common** group on the **Sales and Marketing** area page.

Creating A New Call List

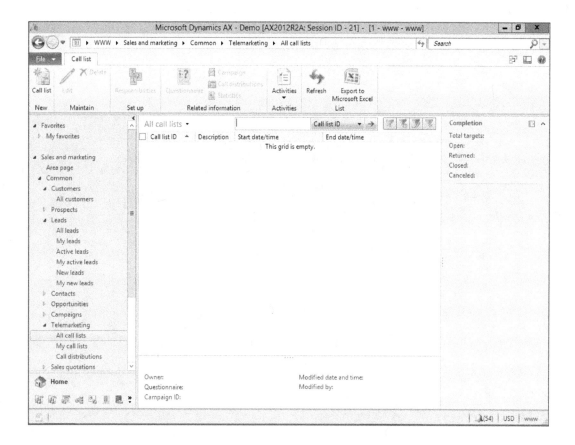

When the **Call List** list page is displayed, click on the **Call List** menu button within the **New** group of the **Call List** ribbon bar.

Creating A New Call List

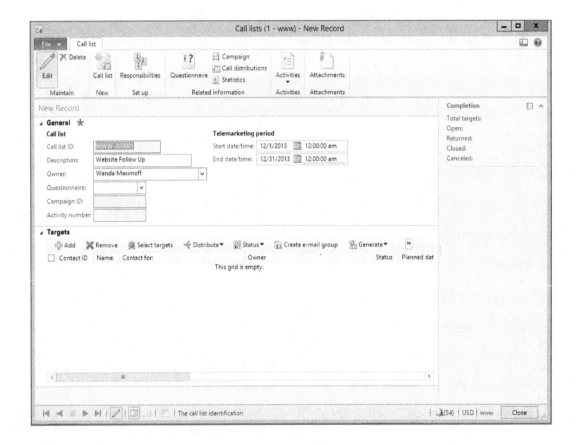

When the **Call List** maintenance form is displayed, give your **Call List** a **Description** and also a **Start date/time**, and **End date/time.**

Expand the **Targets** tab and click on the **Select targets** button within the tab's menu bar to start building your call list targets.

Creating A New Call List

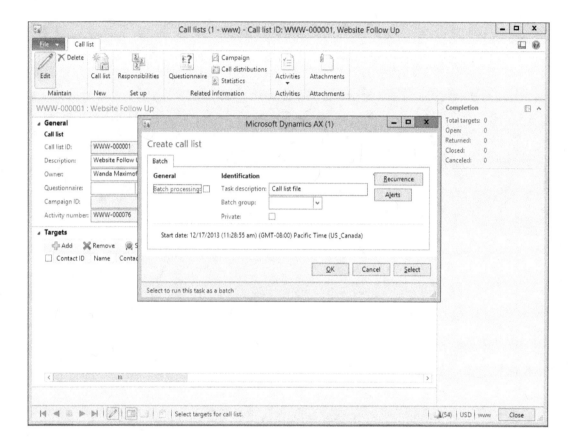

When the **Create call list** dialog box is displayed, click on the **Select** button in the bottom right to build your selection query.

Creating A New Call List

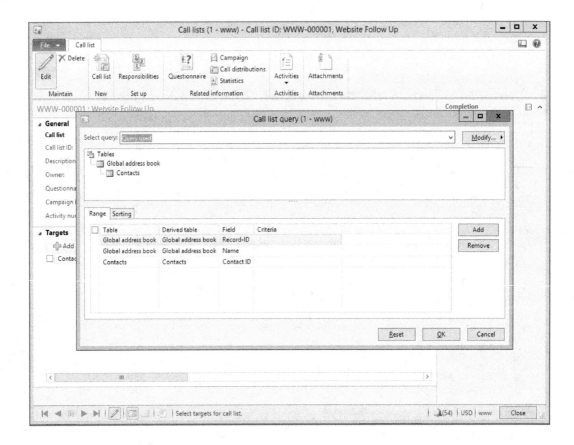

When the **Call list query** designer is displayed you will be able to add additional fields to your search query, and also assign wild cards and selections to the fields to restrict the returned results.

When you have finished updating your query, just click the **OK** button.

Creating A New Call List

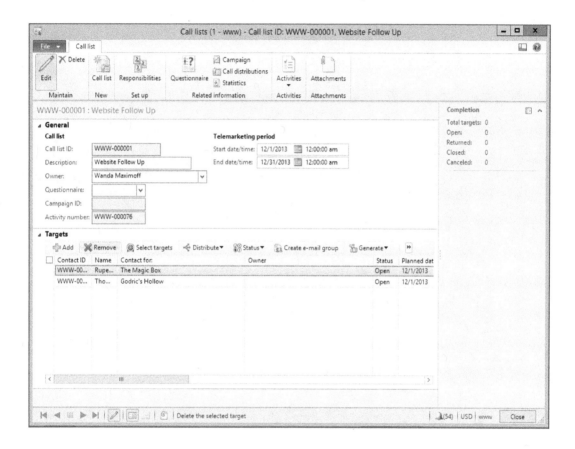

You will now see all of the matching **Contacts** have been added to the Targets of the **Call List.**

Creating A Call List From An Existing Campaigns

Another option that is available for creating **Call Lists** is to generate them directly from your **Campaigns**. This is a much easier process since you have already created a Target audience that you want to contact. All you need to do is click a few buttons, and it will be done.

In this example we will show how you can create **Call Lists** directly from existing **Campaigns**.

Creating A Call List From An Existing Campaigns

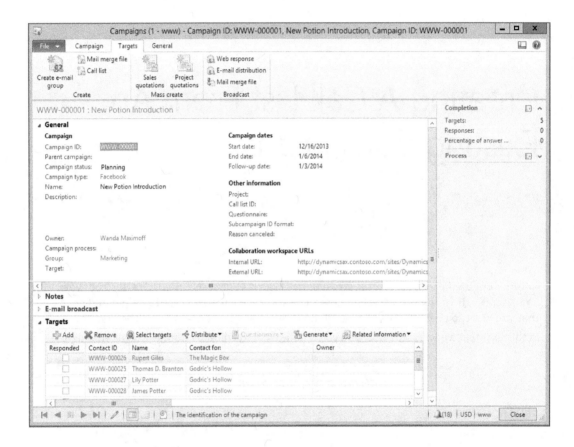

Open up the **Campaign** that you want to create the **Call List** from, and then click on the **Cal list** menu button within the **Create** group of the **Targets** ribbon bar.

Creating A Call List From An Existing Campaigns

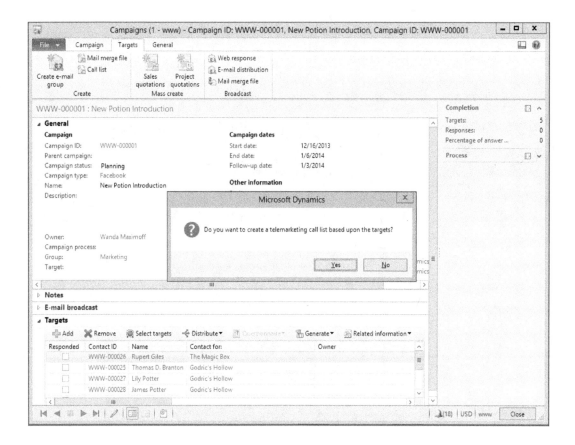

When the confirmation dialog box is displayed asking if you really want to create the **Call List**, click the **Yes** button.

Creating A Call List From An Existing Campaigns

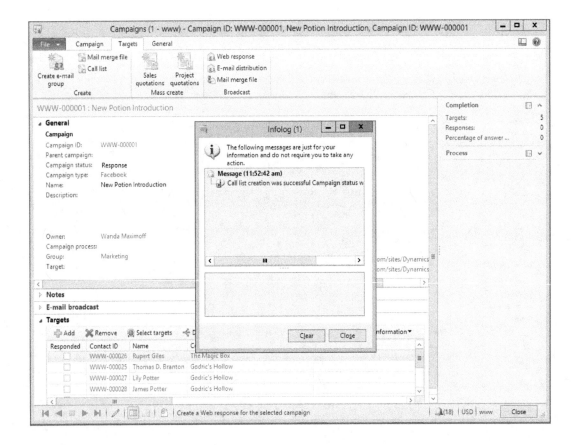

You will then get a confirmation that your **Call List** has been created.

Creating A Call List From An Existing Campaigns

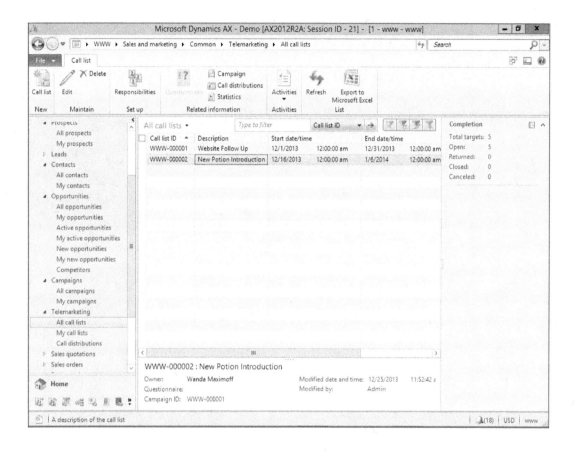

If you return to the **All Call Lists** list page, you will see the new call list that was created.

Creating A Call List From An Existing Campaigns

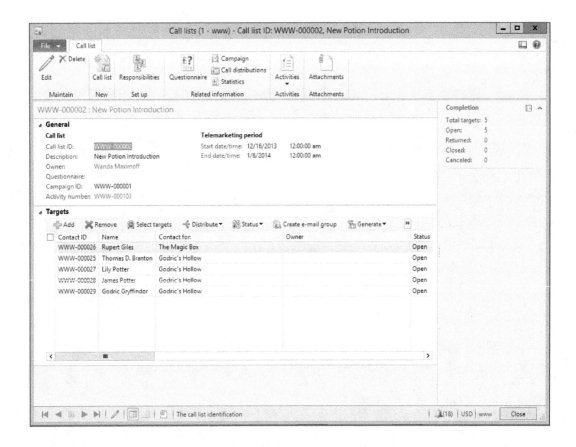

And if you open up the **Call List** then you will see all if the targets from the **Campaign** will be assigned to the **Call List** as well.

Distributing Call List Targets To Responsible Employees

If you have multiple employees that are responsible for your accounts, then when you create a **Call List**, the accounts that are selected will probably be associated with a number of Account Representative. The good thing is that Dynamics AX will allow you to divide up the call list based on the Account Representative that is responsible for the account, and then allow them to work through the call list independently, and at the same time.

In this example we will show how you can distribute the target accounts on the **Call List** to the **Responsible Employees.**

Distributing Call List Targets To Responsible Employees

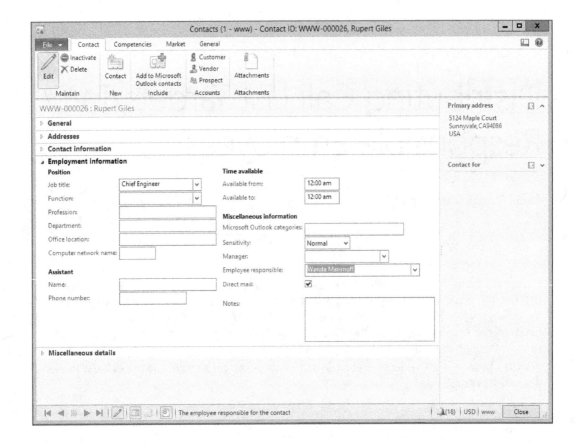

Before you start, there may be some house keeping that you need to do. Some or all of your Contacts, Leads, Prospects, and Customers will need to have a default **Employee Responsible** assigned to them.

Distributing Call List Targets To Responsible Employees

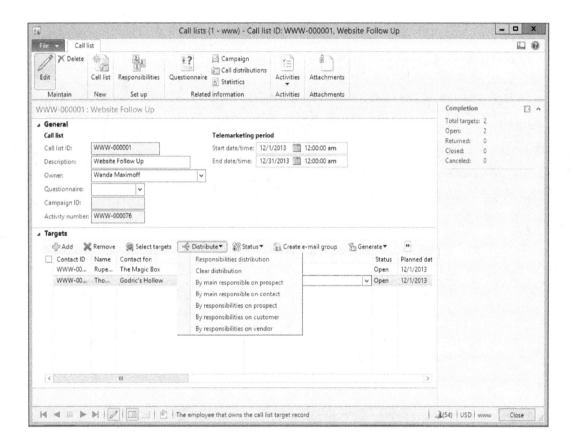

Select the **Call List** that you would like to distribute the work over and then from within the **Targets** tab, click on the **Distribute** menu button within the tabs menu bar, and select the method that you would like to distribute the **Call List** targets.

Distributing Call List Targets To Responsible Employees

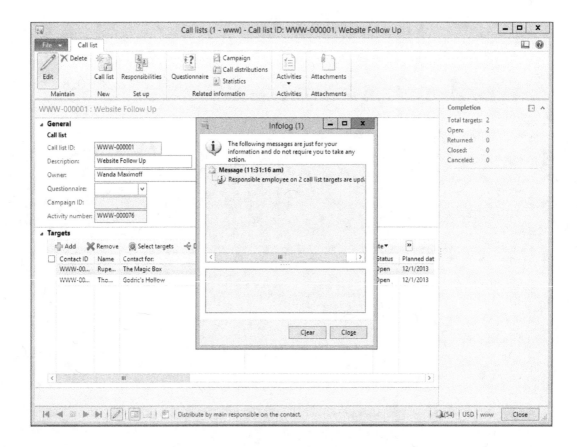

When this is done, you should receive a notification that the targets have been assigned to the employees.

Distributing Call List Targets To Responsible Employees

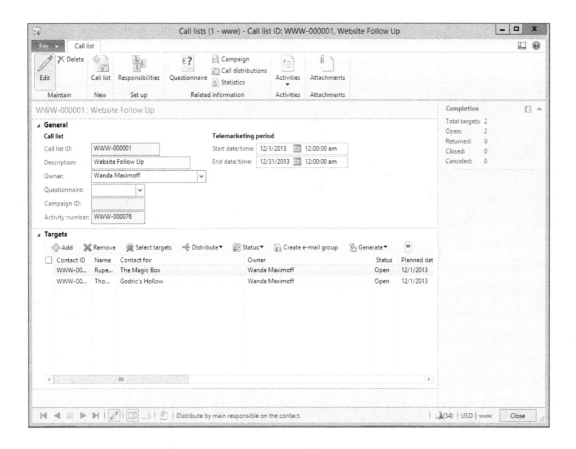

When you return to the **Call List**, you will see that the target accounts now have an **Owner** assigned to them based on the assignment rules that you set up.

Viewing A Users Current Call List Distribution Accounts

Once Target Accounts have been assigned to the Account Representatives, they can access them through their own personal **Call List Distribution** view. This gives them one single location that they can see all of the calls that hey may need to make spanning all of the active **Call Lists**.

In this example we will show how to view a users currently assigned **Call List Distributions**.

Viewing A Users Current Call List Distribution Accounts

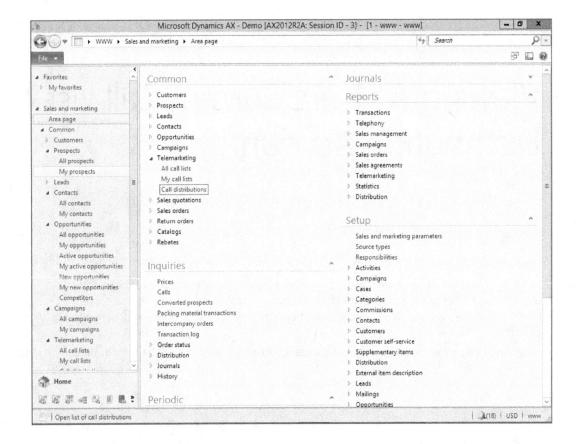

Click on the **Call Distributions** menu item within the **Telemarketing** folder of the **Common** group of the **Sales and Marketing** area page.

Viewing A Users Current Call List Distribution Accounts

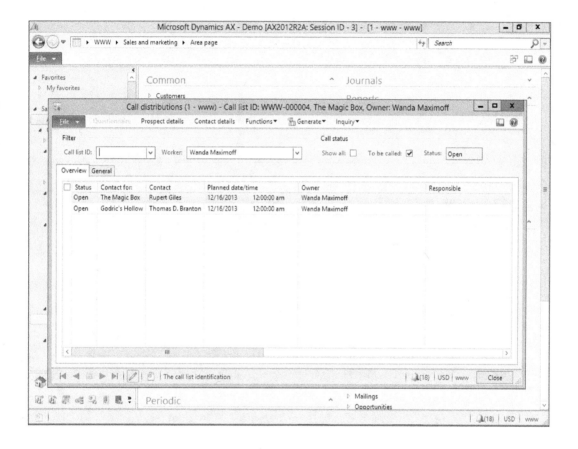

When the **Call Distributions** view is displayed, the user will see all of the assigned accounts that they have been assigned through the **Call Lists.**

Creating Opportunities from Call Distribution Lists

As Account Representatives work though their call lists, they may want to create **Opportunities** associated with the account that they are talking to at the time. Fortunately they can do this easily from their **Call List Distribution** view without having to leave the screen.

In this example we will show how to create an **Opportunity** directly from the **Call Distribution** form.

Creating Opportunities from Call Distribution Lists

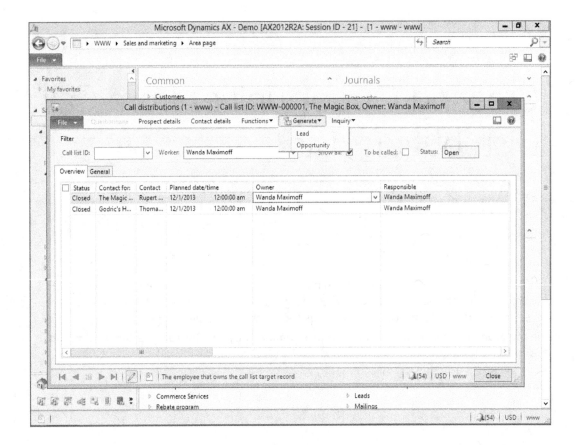

From the **Call Distributions** form, select the account that you would like to create an Opportunity from, click on the **Generate** button in the menu bar, and then select the **Opportunity** menu item.

Creating Opportunities from Call Distribution Lists

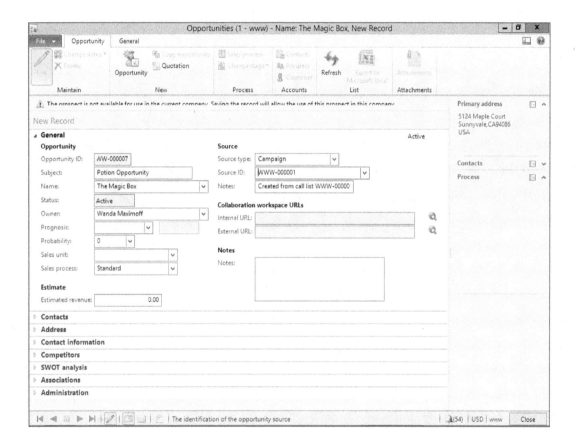

This will immediately create the **Opportunity** for you. Once you have updated the **Opportunity** you can click the **Close** button and return to the **Call Distribution** form.

CONFIGURING CALL LIST SCRIPTS USING QUESTIONNAIRES

Dynamics AX has a feature called **Questionnaires** which allows you to create your own questionnaire formats, with as many questions, and different types of answers that you may want. This feature is integrated into the **Call Lists** giving you a great way to create guided **Call List Scripts** for the **Telemarketers** and as a side effect, all of the responses that are recorded during the **Call List** processing is recorded so that you can create analysis are reports after they have been completed.

In this chapter we will show how you can configure **Questionnaires** and use them within the **Call Lists**.

Defining Question Types

The first step in creating a **Questionnaire** is to define all of the **Question Types** that we will be using within it. The **Question Types** give us an easy way to classify all of the **Questions** later on. In this example we will show how to define valid **Question Types.**

Defining Question Types

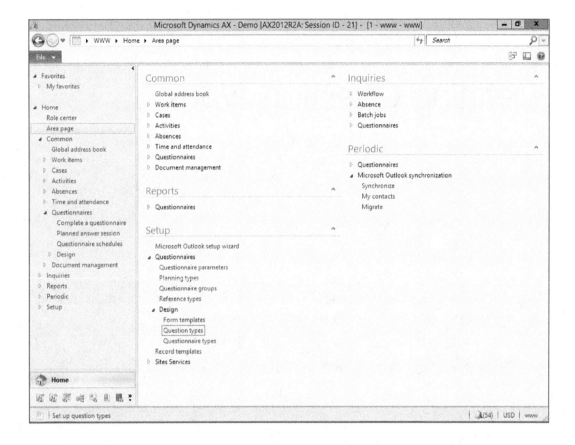

Click on the **Question Types** menu item within the **Design** folder of the **Setup** group within the **Home** area page.

Defining Question Types

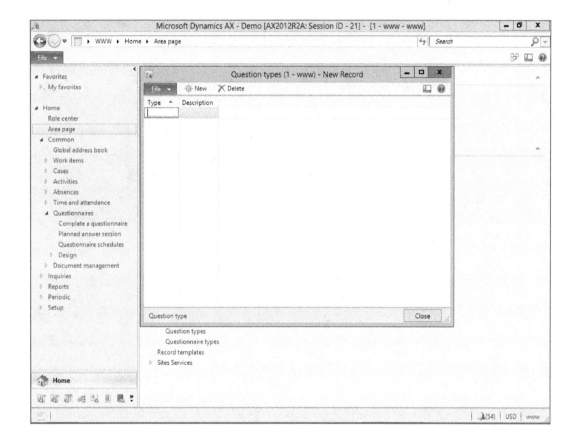

When the **Question Types** maintenance form is displayed, click on the **New** button in the menu bar to add a new record.

Defining Question Types

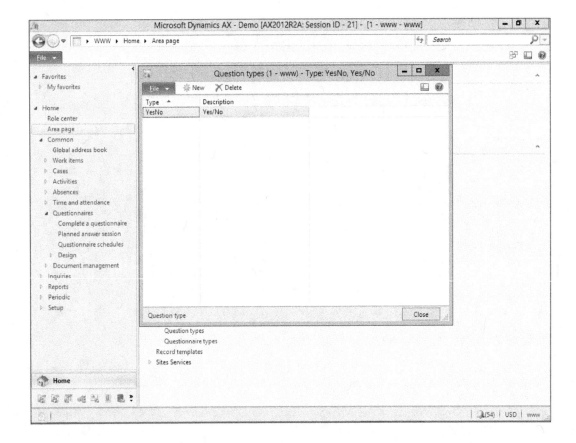

When you have finished setting up your **Question Types** click on the **Close** button to exit the form.

Defining Answer Groups

The next step is to define all of the different **Answer Groups** that we will be associating with **Questions**. **Answer Groups** can be shared over multiple **Questions** which allows us to use them as answer templates.

In this example we will show how you can define your standard **Answer Groups.**

Defining Answer Groups

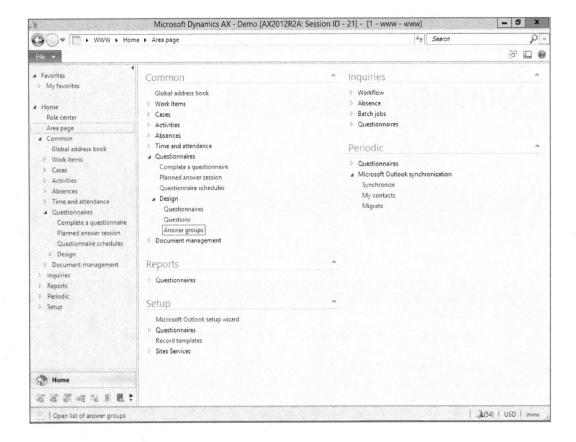

Click on the **Answer Groups** menu item within the **Design** sub-folder of the **Questionnaire** folder of the **Setup** group within the **Home** area page.

Defining Answer Groups

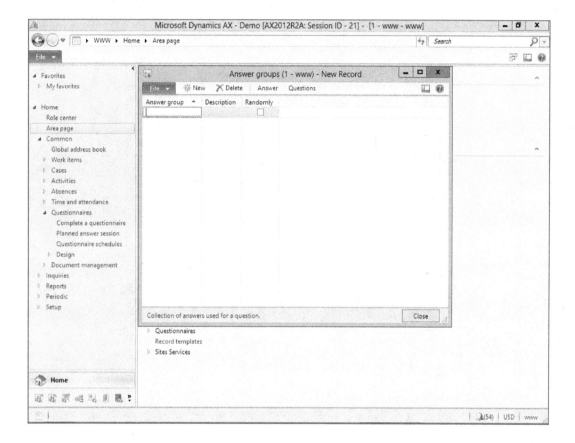

When the **Answer Group** maintenance form is displayed, click on the **New** button in the menu bar to add a new record.

Defining Answer Groups

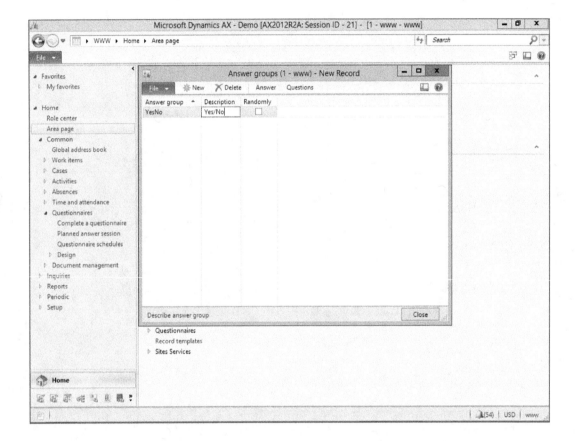

Give your **Answer Group** a name and a **Description.**

You can repeat this process for all the different **Answer Groups** that you may want to use, and when you are finished click the **Close** button to exit from the form.

Defining Valid Answer Group Answers

Answer Groups can also have a set of pre-defined **Answers** associated with them. This ensures that only the valid answer responses are used within the questions, and also has additional features like answer points that can be used for scoring the answers.

In this example we will show how to define a set of standard **Answers** for an **Answer Group.**

Defining Answer Groups

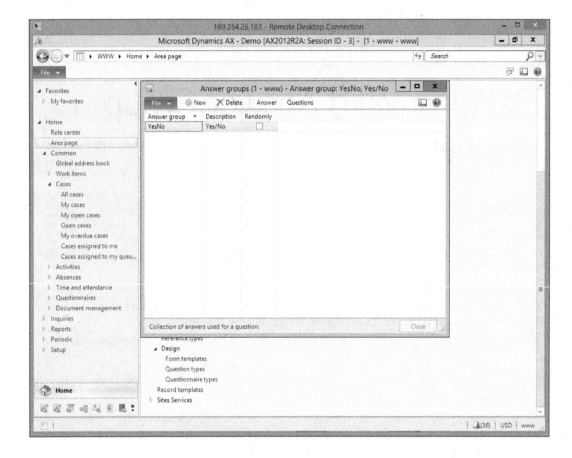

Select the **Answer Group** that you would like to specify the answers for and then click on the **Answer** button within the menu bar.

Defining Answer Groups

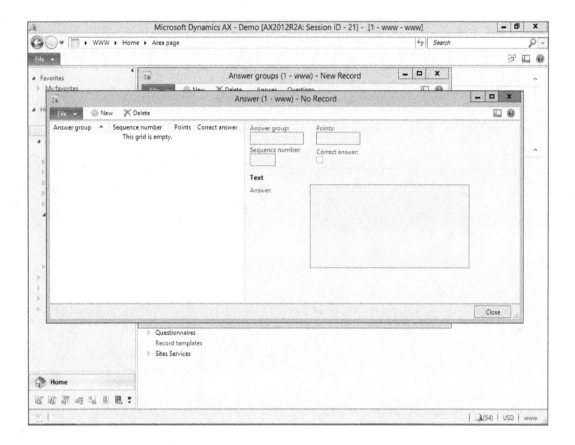

When the **Answer** maintenance form is displayed, click on the **New** button on the menu bar to create a new **Answer** record.

Defining Answer Groups

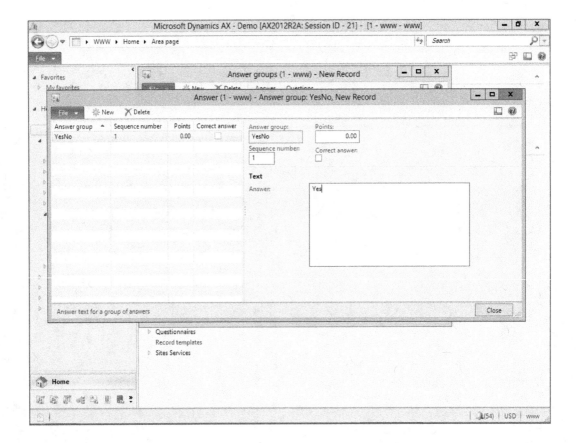

Then set an **Answer** for the record.

Defining Answer Groups

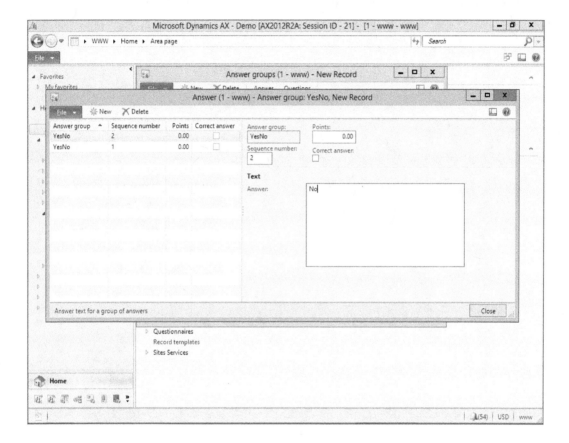

Repeat the process for all of the other valid **Answers**, and when you are finished click the **Close** button to exit from the form.

Configuring Questions

Once you have defined your **Question Types**, and **Answer Types** you can build your standard **Questions** that you want to use within your **Questionnaires**. These are going to be template questions, and you can use them over and over again within as many **Questionnaires** as you like.

In this example we will show how to configure your template **Questions.**

Configuring Questions

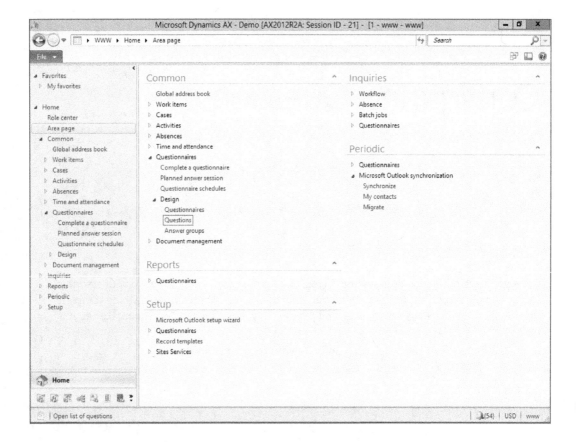

Click on the **Questions** menu item within the **Design** sub-folder of the **Questionnaire** folder of the **Setup** group within the **Home** area page.

Configuring Questions

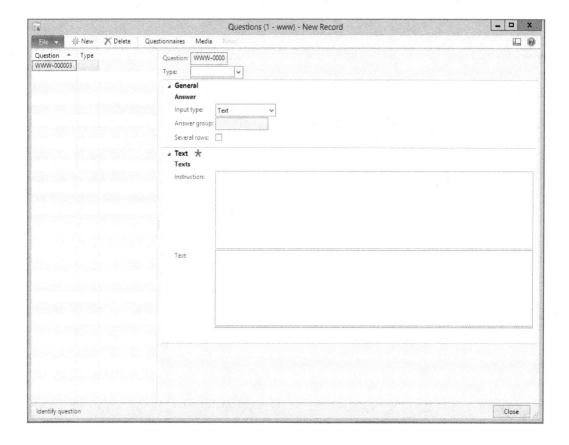

When the **Questions** maintenance form is displayed, click on the **New** menu button to create a new **Question.**

Configuring Questions

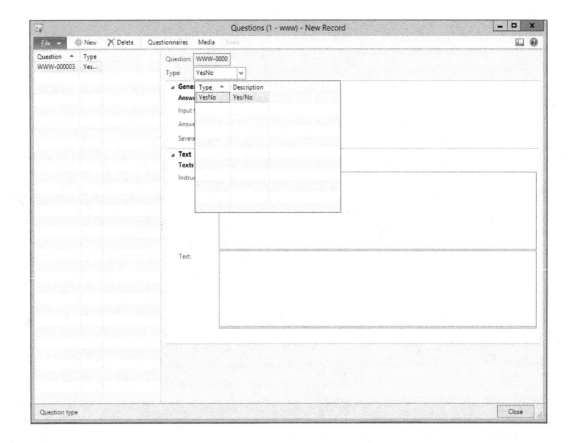

Select the **Type** of answer that you would like to use for the **Question** from the list of **Question Types** that you have configured.

Configuring Questions

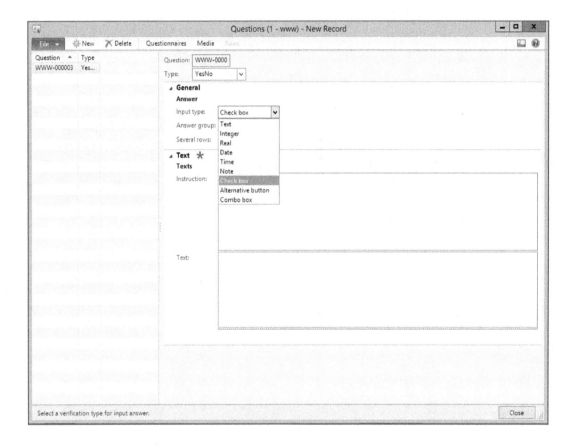

Then select the **Input Type** for the **Question** that you want to use for the **Answer.**

Configuring Questions

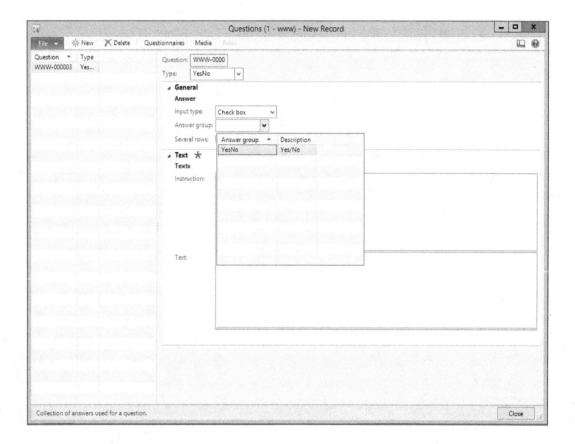

Then select the **Answer Group** that you would like to use for the question from the list of **Answer Groups** that you have configured.

Configuring Questions

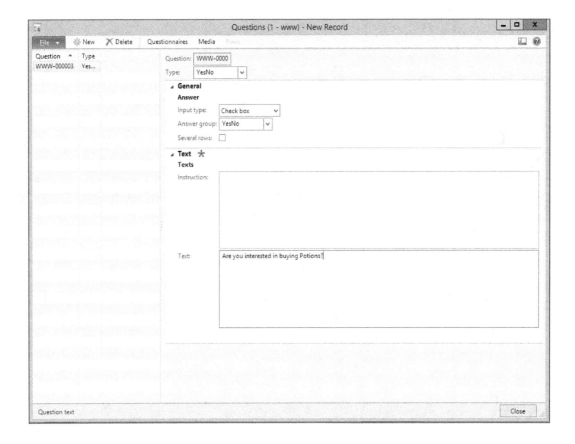

Then within the **Text** field type in the question text that you want to use when the **Question** is used.

Note: If you also want to add some **Instruction** text, then this could be used to further scripting notes.

Configuring Questions

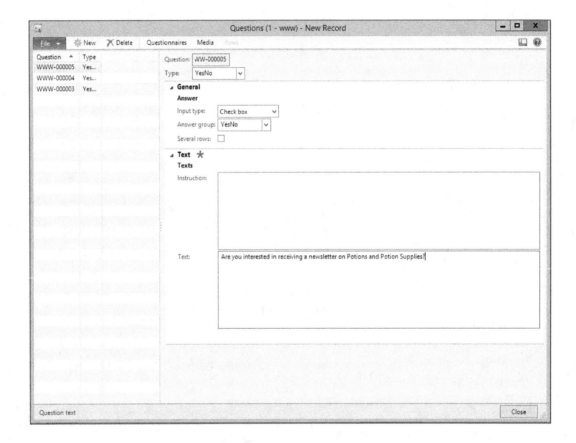

Continue adding additional **Questions** and when you are finished, click on the **Close** button to exit the form.

Defining Questionnaire Types

Now we will define the **Questionnaire Types** that we will use to classify our **Questionnaires**. This allows us to group common **Questionnaires** together for reporting purposes, and also gives us a great way to quickly search through them for the types that we are looking for.

In this example we will show how to define **Questionnaire Types.**

Defining Questionnaire Types

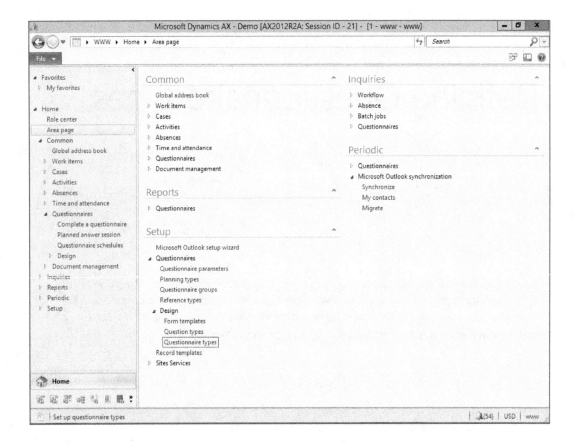

Click on the **Questionnaire Types** menu item within the **Design** folder of the **Setup** group within the **Home** area page.

Defining Questionnaire Types

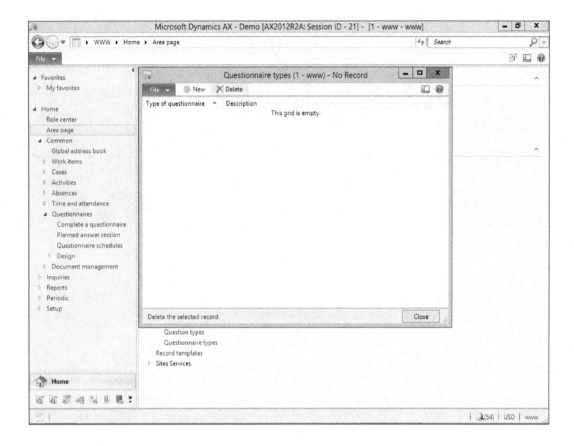

When the **Questionnaire Types** maintenance form is displayed, click on the **New** button in the menu bar to add a new record.

Defining Questionnaire Types

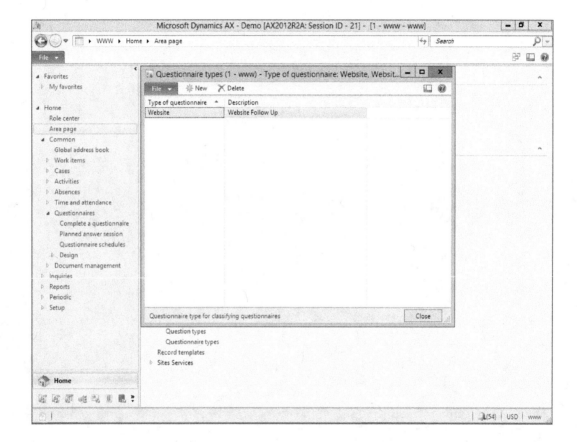

When you have finished setting up your **Questionnaire Types** click on the **Close** button to exit the form.

Configuring a Questionnaire

Once all of the foundation has been laid for the **Questionnaires**, you can start building your Telemarketing Scripts.

In this example we will show how to create a new **Questionnaire** for your scripts.

Configuring a Questionnaire

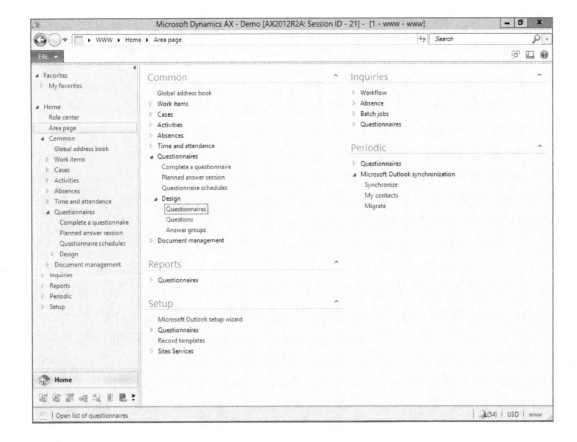

Click on the **Questionnaires** menu item within the **Design** sub-folder of the **Questionnaire** folder of the **Setup** group within the **Home** area page.

Configuring a Questionnaire

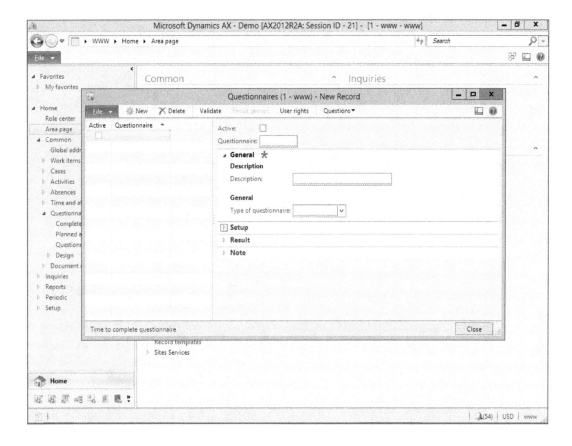

When the **Questionnaires** maintenance form is displayed, click on the **New** menu button to create a new **Questionnaire.**

Configuring a Questionnaire

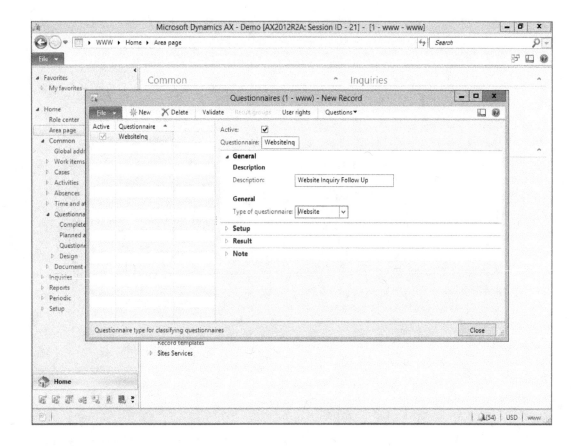

Give your **Questionnaire** a name, a short **Description** and also assign it a **Questionnaire Type.**

Configuring a Questionnaire

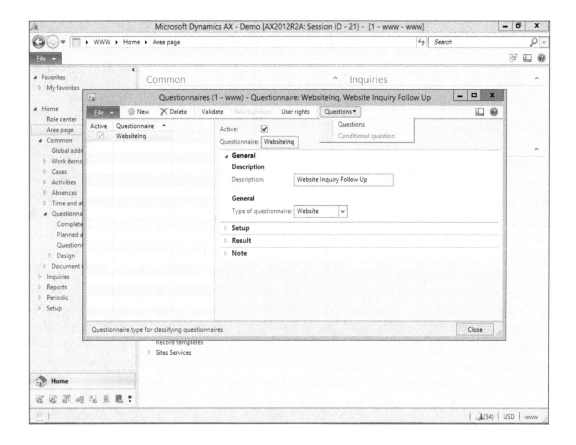

To assign **Questions** to your **Questionnaire**, click on the **Questions** button within the menu bar, and select the **Questions** menu item.

Configuring a Questionnaire

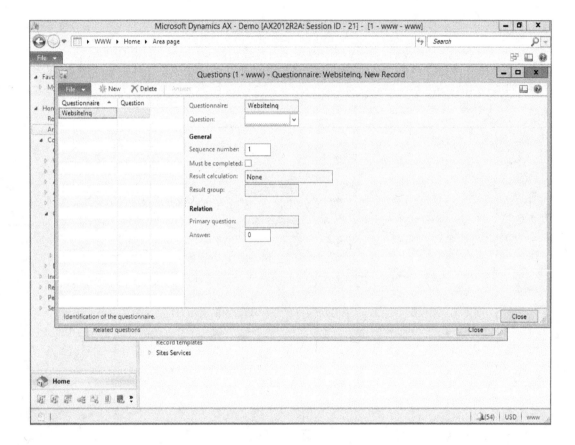

When the **Questions** maintenance form is displayed, click on the **New** button on the menu bar to create a new **Question** record.

Configuring a Questionnaire

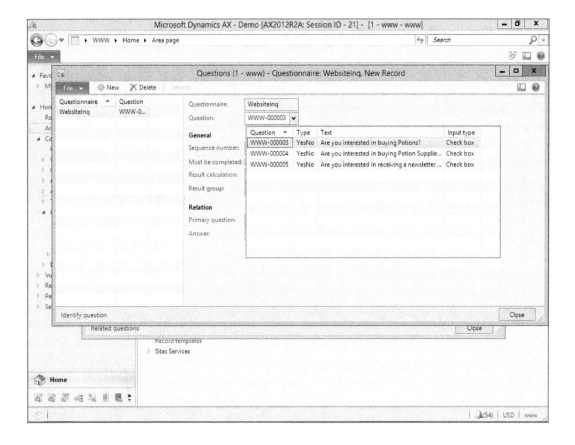

From the **Question** dropdown field, select the **Question** template that you would like to use.

Configuring a Questionnaire

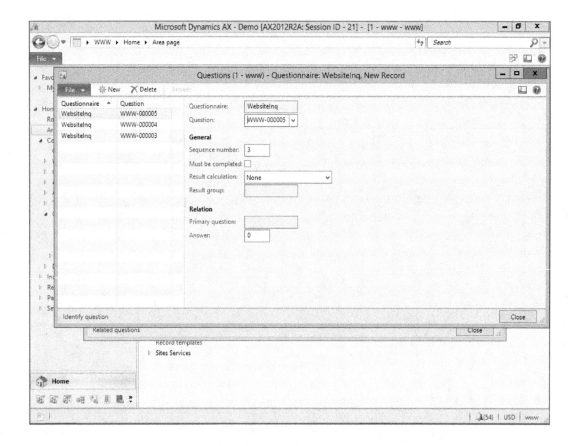

Repeat the process for all of the other **Questions** that you would like to use and then click the **Close** button to exit the form.

Assigning a Questionnaire to a Call List

The final step in this process is to assign your **Questionnaire** to your **Call Lists** so that the users will be able to kick them off as they are calling the accounts.

In this example we will show how you assign a **Questionnaire** to a **Call List.**

Assigning a Questionnaire to a Call List

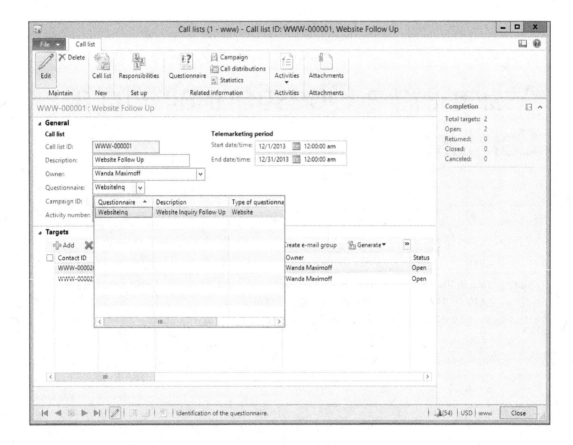

Open up the **Call List** that you would like to assign the **Questionnaire** to and select it from the **Questionnaire** drop down within the **General** tab.

Using Questionnaires While Processing Call Lists

Once the **Questionnaire** has been assigned to the **Call List** the users have the ability to start the **Questionnaire** running directly from the **Call Distribution** screen.

In this example we will show how to execute a **Questionnaire** from the **Call Distribution** function.

Using Questionnaires While Processing Call Lists

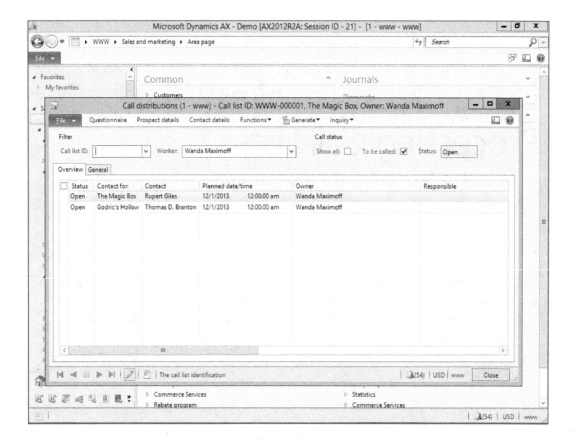

Open up the **Call Distributions** form select the **Contact** that you would like to perform the **Questionnaire** on, and click the **Questionnaire** button within the menu bar.

Using Questionnaires While Processing Call Lists

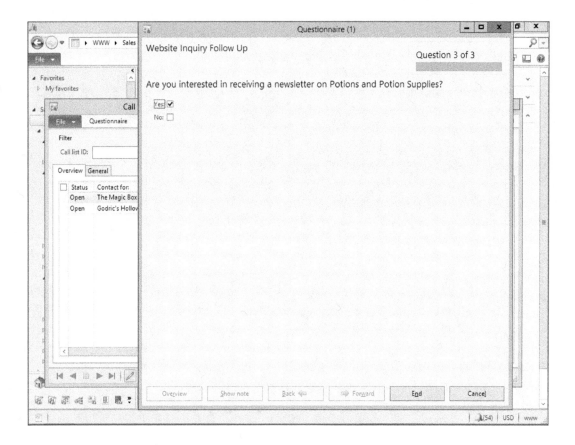

This will start off a **Questionnaire** and step you through each of the questions tracking the answers as you go.

After you have answered all of the questions then you can exit out of the **Questionnaire** by clicking on the **End** button.

SUMMARY

In this guide we have shown a lot of the CRM features that are included in the **Sales and Marketing** area of Dynamics AX. This is not the extent of what you can do though. You will notice that there are other features that you might want to look at. They include:

- **Workflows** – These can be used to add addition routings and controls around **Cases.**
- **Portal Access** – Almost all of the functions that we described in this blueprint are accessible through the web portal, giving you on the go access.
- **Customer Self Service** – Customers can be granted access to the Self Service Portal and update their own information.
- **Email Templates** – In our examples, we just sent out simple e-mails through marketing, but these can be templatized to make it look a little more professional.
- **Prospect and Lead Imports** – If you buy Leads and Prospects, then you can import them in from files automatically, saving you a lot of manual data entry.
- **Duplicate Checking** – You can de-duplicate and merge records directly from the Global Address Book, making it easier to cleanse your imported Leads and Prospects.

Before you start off down the road of searching for a CRM system to bolt onto Dynamics AX, take a look at what you already have. You might find that it does everything that you need.

About the Author

Murray Fife is a Microsoft Dynamics AX MVP, Author, and Solution Architect at I.B.I.S. Inc with over 18 years of experience in the software industry.

Like most people in this industry he has paid his dues as a developer, an implementation consultant, a trainer, and now spend most of his days working with companies solving their problems with the Microsoft suite of products, specializing in the Dynamics® AX solutions.

Founded in 1989, I.B.I.S., Inc. (www.ibisinc.com) provides distributors and manufacturers with next-generation supply chain solutions to maximize their profitability. A winning combination of industry and supply chain expertise, world-class supply chain software developed in partnership with distributors and manufacturers, and 25 years of successful Microsoft Dynamics implementations has culminated in making I.B.I.S., Inc. the preferred Microsoft Dynamics partner and solution provider for distributors and manufacturers worldwide.

EMAIL	murray@murrayfife.me
TWITTER	@murrayfife
SKYPE	murrayfife
AMAZON	http://www.amazon.com/author/murrayfife
BLOG	http://dynamicsaxtipoftheday.com http://extendingdynamicsax.com http://atinkerersnotebook.com
SLIDESHARE	http://slideshare.net/murrayfife
LINKEDIN	http://www.linkedin.com/in/murrayfife

www.ingramcontent.com/pod-product-compliance
Lightning Source LLC
LaVergne TN
LVHW062259060326
832902LV00013B/1963